RESURRECTION
AND IMMORTALITY

RESURRECTION
AND
IMMORTALITY

A selection from the
Drew Lectures on Immortality

EDITED BY
CHARLES S. DUTHIE

SAMUEL BAGSTER & SONS LTD

LONDON

Samuel Bagster & Sons Ltd.
a member of the Pentos group
1 Bath Street, London EC1V 9LB

Copyright © The Trustees of the Drew Lectureship,
Spurgeon's College, London 1979

First published 1979

British Library CIP data
Resurrection and immortality
   1. Immortality – Addresses, essays, lectures
   I. Duthie, Charles, Sim
   236′.22′08   BT923

ISBN 0–85150–307–1
Printed in Great Britain by
Butler & Tanner Ltd,
Frome and London

Contents

Contents

Contributors

WILLIAM TEMPLE (1881–1944). Archbishop of York, 1929–1942; Archbishop of Canterbury, 1942–1944. *Mens Creatrix*, 1917; *Christus Veritas*, 1924; *Nature, Man and God*, 1934; *Readings in St John's Gospel*, 1939; *Christianity and the Social Order*, 1942.

SYDNEY CAVE (1883–1953). President, Cheshunt College, 1923–1933; Principal, New College, University of London, 1933–1953. *An Introduction to the Study of Some Living Religions of the East*, 1921; *The Doctrine of the Person of Christ*, 1925; *Christianity and Some Living Religions of the East*, 1929; *The Doctrine of the Work of Christ*, 1937; *The Christian Way*, 1949.

T. W. MANSON (1893–1958). Rylands Professor of Biblical Criticism and Exegesis, University of Manchester, 1936–1958. *The Teaching of Jesus*, 1931; *The Mission and Message of Jesus* (with H. D. A. Major and C. J. Wright), 1937; *The Church's Ministry*, 1948; *The Sayings of Jesus*, 1949; *The Beginning of the Gospel*, 1950.

H. T. ANDREWS (1864–1928). Professor of Church History and Historical Theology, Cheshunt College, 1895–1903; Professor of New Testament Exegesis and Criticism, New College, University of London, 1903–1928. *The Acts of the Apostles*, 1908; *The Apocryphal Books of the Old and New Testament*, 1908; *The Value of the Theology of St Paul for Modern Thought, 1914*; *The Christ of Apostolic Faith*, 1929.

C. K. BARRETT (1917–   ). Professor of Divinity, University of Durham, 1958–   ). *The Holy Spirit and the Gospel Tradition*, 1947; *The Gospel according to St John*, 1955; *The Epistle to the Romans*, 1957; *The Pastoral Epistles*, 1963; *The First Epistle to the Corinthians*, 1968; *The Second Epistle to the Corinthians*, 1973.

G. B. CAIRD (1917–   ) Senior Tutor, Mansfield College, Oxford, 1959–1970 and Principal, 1970–1977; Dean Ireland's Professor of Exegesis of Holy Scripture, 1977–   . *The Truth of the Gospel*, 1950; *Principalities and Powers*, 1956; *The Gospel According to St Luke*, 1963; *The Revelation of St John the Divine*, 1966; *Paul's Letters from Prison*, 1976.

Contributors

G. R. BEASLEY-MURRAY (1916–   ) Principal, Spurgeon's College, London, 1958–1973; Professor of New Testament Interpretation, Southern Baptist Theological Seminary, Louisville, 1973–   . *Baptism and the New Testament*, 1962; *The Ressurection of Jesus Christ*, 1964; *The Book of Revelation*, 1974.

H. CUNLIFFE-JONES (1905–   ) Principal, Yorkshire United Independent College, 1947–1958; Associate Principal, Northern Congregational College, 1958–1966; Professor, History of Doctrine, 1966–1968, then Professor of Theology, 1968–1973, University of Manchester. *The Holy Spirit*, 1943; *The Authority of the Biblical Revelation*, 1945; *Deuteronomy*, 1951; *Jeremiah*, 1960; *Technology, Community and Church*, 1961; *Christian Theology since 1600*, 1970.

H. F. LOVELL COCKS (1894–   ). Professor of Systematic Theology, Yorkshire United Independent College, 1932–1937; Principal, Scottish Congregational College, 1937–1941; Principal, Western College, 1941–1960. *By Faith Alone*, 1943; *The Nonconformist Conscience*, 1943; *The Wondrous Cross*, 1957; *The Religious Life of Oliver Cromwell*, 1960.

A. M. RAMSEY (1904–   ) Archbishop of York, 1956–1961; Archbishop of Canterbury, 1961–1974. *The Gospel and the Catholic Church*, 1936; *The Resurrection of Christ*, 1945; *From Gore to Temple*, 1960; *Canterbury Essays and Addresses*, 1964; *Canterbury Pilgrims*, 1974; *Holy Spirit*, 1977.

PETER BARRACLOUGH (1925–   ) Minister; Hampstead Garden Suburb Free Church, 1961–   ; previously minister at Caerphilly and Ipswich.

CHARLES S. DUTHIE (1911–   ) Principal, Scottish Congregational College, 1944–1964 and lecturer, Post-graduate School of Theology, University of Edinburgh, 1946–1964; Principal, New College, University of London, 1964–1977. *God in His World*, 1955; *Outline of Christian Belief*, 1968.

Preface

What has come to be known as the Drew Lecture on Immortality was founded in 1907 by Mr John Drew of Haringey Park, Middlesex. It was his wish that 'instruction, assurance and inspiration should be given as to the soul's destiny and as to the nature and reality of life hereafter, directly or indirectly in the interest of personal immortality'. Until 1977 the Drew Trust was administered by a committee consisting of the theological teachers and officers of New College, London. When at the end of September of that year New College ceased to function as a theological college preparing men and women for the Christian ministry and as a School of Divinity of the University of London, the Trust was handed over to a similar committee of Spurgeon's College, thus making it possible for the lecture to continue to be delivered in London, as Mr Drew desired.

There are good reasons for believing that this is an opportune moment to present to the public a selection from the rich material provided by the Drew lectures. After years of comparative neglect the idea of personal immortality is again claiming the attention of Christian and non-Christian thinkers alike. Our growing concern with the subject of death forces us to ask whether the brief span of human life on earth, broken in its first promise or shadowed by suffering for so many, makes sense in itself or cries out rather for a fulfilling sequel. The question sharpens in the continuing debate between Christianity, with its dual emphasis on a new quality of life both here and hereafter, and optimistic secular philosophies which, in face of human perversity, are driven to acknowledge that even a mild golden age to come cannot be guaranteed. In this discussion the Christian faith has a distinctive word to speak. William Temple puts it clearly and succinctly in the very first lecture: 'Man is not immortal by nature or of right; but there is offered to him resurrection from the dead and life eternal if he will receive it from God and on God's terms.'

It has not been an easy task to make the final selection necessary for this volume from the varied wealth available; but the task has been made lighter by the invaluable work done by Dr Herbert Hartwell several years ago. He examined and analysed the lectures published up to 1968 and suggested three different schemes as possible candidates for publication. I have profited greatly from Dr Hartwell's proposals in making my own choice. Two main principles have guided that choice. The first is that a book consisting mainly of essays by scholarly writers who are daily engaged in the study of the Bible and of theology is more likely to be of value and of use than a book based upon another principle of selection. A Christian doctrine of eternal life must have a solid foundation. Let me add that although the majority of contributors have either been or still are theological teachers, what they have written is not for scholars only. A lively faith in God, which is the source of the Christian hope, undergirds and is indeed visible in all they say. I must confess, however, to a genuine regret that it has not been possible, with one exception, to include in the present volume some of the excellent lectures given by notable preachers. Their essays could well form another book.

The second guiding principle has been the desirability of some kind of order or progression in the series of lectures offered. It is obvious that a selection of essays written over a long period of years by writers free to choose their own topics cannot be expected to achieve the coverage and coherence attainable in a symposium on the same general theme presented by a group of contemporaries. On the other hand, while there is a certain amount of understandable overlapping, the Drew lecturers were aware of what had been written by their predecessors and sought either to break new ground or to look at old ground with fresh eyes. This is particularly evident in the treatment of the biblical material. The wide range of the field covered has in fact made it possible to construct a reasonable and, it is to be hoped, a helpful order of lectures.

The opening essay by William Temple, written with his characteristic grasp and lucidity, makes a useful introduction by raising fundamental issues and by indicating the main lines of a Christian doctrine of immortality. Sydney Cave's treatment of reincarnation, which follows, owes its cogency to his early familiarity *in situ* with the religions of India. The interested reader may wish to compare it with the more extended handling of the same subject by John Hick in his recent book *Death and Eternal Life* (Collins, 1976). The five lectures which follow are directly concerned with the Bible and, for the most part, with the New Testament. Admirers of the late T. W. Manson will be glad to find his valuable essay introducing this section. It is appropriately succeeded by H. T. Andrew's sketch of the teaching of Jesus on the future life. Next comes, almost at mid-point, the crucial essay of C. K. Barrett on the much debated question about the relation between the idea of resurrection and the idea of immortality. This is, I venture to say, one of the most significant lectures in the book. If justification be required for the inclusion of the Epistle to the Hebrews and the Book of Revelation it can surely be found in the intrinsic merit of the imaginative essays by G. B. Caird and G. R. Beasley-Murray. A full treatment of the thought of Paul on life after death has not been included partly because its main features are sufficiently well known and partly because a central aspect of it is taken up in C. K. Barrett's lecture.

Following upon the section of lectures upon biblical material are three essays which deal with man's destiny beyond the present life. If we are to be true to the wholeness of New Testament thought the reality of judgement after

death must be taken seriously and not dismissed as outmoded
or irrelevant or incompatible with the nature of a loving
God. H. Cunliffe-Jones offers such a serious appraisal. Lovell
Cocks then affirms the positive side of the Christian expectation in his persuasive theological meditation on 'The Hope
of Glory'. Last but by no means least we have A. M. Ramsey's reflections on 'Heaven and Hell'. Here Christian
thought and Christian devotion unite to face an issue that
cannot be avoided.

The selection might well have ended at this point – with
one archbishop as it began with another! I felt, however,
that the book required for its completion first of all a lecture
of a practical and pastoral kind. This need is well served
by the Rev Peter Barraclough's 'Immortality and Bereavement' which considers the shattering effect of death on those
who lose loved ones and long to be sure of continuance and
reunion in a life beyond. My own Drew lecture 'Ultimate
Triumph' forms, I am told, a suitable conclusion, urging,
as it does, the final, universal victory of God's love in Christ
even if the shadow cast by the possibility of continuing
human resistance remains to remind us of our responsibility
to give a personal answer, a 'Yes' or a 'No', to the divine
grace.

The theme that recurs throughout these twelve lectures
is that human immortality is the gift of God whose power
alone can enable the human self to continue after death in
order that it may enjoy fellowship with him in company with
others. The appropriate title for the book seems therefore to
be 'Resurrection and Immortality'.

CHARLES S. DUTHIE

The Idea of Immortality
in Relation to Religion
and Ethics

WILLIAM TEMPLE

It is not easy to estimate the place which the idea of immortality now holds in the actual religion of English people. Certainly it is nothing like so prominent as it has been in most previous ages of Christian history. And so far as it plays a part, it is a very different part. Here as in other departments of life we find ourselves at the end of a period of reaction from the middle ages. The medieval scheme, still presented by the Roman Catholic Church, is entirely intelligible in its broad outlines. Universal immortality is assumed; for those who are beyond pardon there is hell; for those who are pardonable, purgatory; for those whose pardon is accomplished, paradise. And alongside of these, for the unawakened soul there is limbo. The scheme presents certain administrative difficulties. It involves, in practice, the drawing of a sharp line between the awakened and the unawakened, and again, between the pardonable and the unpardonable. But unless it be held – as in fact I find myself driven to hold – that these difficulties are insoluble in principle, it may be urged that they are soluble to omniscience, which, *ex hypothesi*, is available for the purpose.

There are many of us, however, to whom the difficulty mentioned is so overwhelming as to make the whole scheme unreal, however water-tight it may be dialectically. And I have not hesitated to speak of it in terms which indicate that sense of unreality. For the human soul is at once too

1

delicately complex, and too closely unified, to be dealt with by any method of classification whatever into mutually exclusive groups. And how can there be paradise for any while there is hell, conceived as unending torment, for some? Each supposedly damned soul was born into the world as a mother's child; and paradise cannot be paradise for her if her child is in such a hell. The scheme is unworkable in practice even by omniscience, and moreover it offends against the deepest Christian sentiments.

But this is a very modern reaction to it. What happened at the Reformation was very different. The doctrine of purgatory was the focus of many grave abuses – sales of indulgences and the like. These called for remedy, and thus set moving the normal method of the Reformers – the method of referring whatever was found to call for remedy to the touchstone of Scripture. And Scripture supplied no basis for a doctrine of purgatory. So the doctrine was not freed from its abuses but was eliminated, and the Protestant world was left with the stark alternatives of heaven and hell.

Now the medieval scheme, being easily intelligible as a theory, however difficult in practice, had great homiletic value. It presented vividly to the imagination the vitally important truth of the 'abiding consequences' of our actions and of the characters that we form. And this homiletic value was if anything increased at first through the simplification effected by the Reformers. There, plain before all men, was the terrible alternative. Only by faith in Christ could a man be delivered from certain torment in hell to the unending bliss of heaven; but by that faith he could have assurance, full and complete, of his deliverance; and that faith would be fruitful in his life and character.

But there was much to set upon the other side. The new form of the scheme gave a new prominence to hell, and whereas the popular mind in the middle ages was mainly concerned with purgatory and with ways of shortening or mitigating its cleansing pains, it was now hell that alone supplied the deterrent influence of belief in a future life. And this, while it lasted, reacted on the conception of God. For punishment which is unending is plainly retributive only in the long run; it may have a deterrent use while this life lasts, but from the Day of Judgement onwards it would lose that quality, and it obviously has no reformative aim. And it requires much ingenuity to save from the charge of vindictiveness a character which inflicts forever a punishment which can be no other than retributive. Certainly the popular conception of God in many Protestant circles became almost purely vindictive. We can read in the protests of such writers as Shelley and Byron what sort of picture of God had been impressed on their imaginations.

> Is there a God? Ay, an almighty God,
> And vengeful as almighty. Once His voice
> Was heard on earth; earth shuddered at the sound;
> The fiery-visaged firmament expressed
> Abhorrence, and the grave of Nature yawned
> To swallow all the dauntless and the good
> That dared to hurl defiance at His throne
> Girt as it was with power.

No doubt Shelley was in violent reaction, and misrepresented by exaggeration what he had been taught, in addition to using the irony of indignation in order to satirize it. Yet a caricature depends for its force on maintaining some resemblance to what it ridicules. And there are sermons of the eighteenth century which go far to justify the poet's indignant contempt.

But such conceptions could not permanently survive in the minds of people who read the Gospels. Steadily the conviction has gained ground that the God and Father of our Lord Jesus Christ cannot be conceived as inflicting on any soul that he has made unending torment. So hell has in effect been banished from popular belief; and as purgatory had been banished long before, we are left with a very widespread sentimental notion that all persons who die are forthwith in paradise or heaven. And this seems to involve a conception of God as so genially tolerant as to be morally indifferent, and converts the belief in immortality from a moral stimulant to a moral narcotic. There is a very strong case for thinking out the whole subject again in as complete independence as possible alike of medieval and of Protestant traditions. The reaction from the middle ages here as elsewhere has worked itself out.

It has often been pointed out that in the religious experience of Israel the hope of immortality is of late origin. In the earlier times there was an expectation of a shadowy existence in Sheol; but it was not a hope. 'O spare me a little that I may recover my strength, before I go hence and be no more seen' is a prayer as far removed as possible from either the later Jewish or the Christian faith in the life to come. The hope of immortality as we understand it only dawned when faith in God as One and as Righteous was already firmly established. Those of us who believe in the providential guidance of Israel's spiritual growth will at once seek a divine purpose in this order of development, but those who start with no such pre-supposition may quite well trace a value in it which has permanent importance.

The great aim of all true religion is to transfer the centre of interest and concern from self to God. Until the doctrine of God in its main elements is really established, it would be definitely dangerous to reach a developed doctrine of immortality. Even when the doctrine of God is established in its Christian form, the doctrine and hope of immortality can still, as experience abundantly shows, perpetuate self-centredness in the spiritual life. If my main concern in relation to things eternal is to be with the question what is going to become of *me*, it might be better that I should have no hope of immortality at all, so that at least as I looked forward into the vista of the ages my Self should not be a possible object of primary concern.

4

William Temple

For as in order of historical development, so also in order of spiritual value, the hope of immortality is strictly dependent on and subordinate to faith in God. If God is righteous – still more, if God is Love – immortality follows as a consequence. He made me; he loves me; he will not let me perish, so long as there is in me anything that he can love. And that is a wholesome reflection for me if, but only if, the result is that I give greater glory to God in the first place, and take comfort to myself only, if at all, in the second place. I wish to stress this heavily. Except as an implicate in the righteousness and love of God, I cannot see that immortality is a primary religious interest at all. It has an interest for us as beings who cling to life, but there is nothing religious about that. It has an interest for us as social beings who love our friends and desire to meet again those who have died before us; that is an interest capable of religious consecration, and for many devout souls it has an exceedingly high religious value; but even this is not religious in itself. No; the centre of all true religious interest is God, and self comes into it not as a primary concern which God must serve, but as that one thing which each can offer for the glory of God. And if it were so, that his glory could best be served by my annihilation – so be it.

But in fact God is known to us through his dealings with us. And if he left us to perish with hopes frustrated and purposes unaccomplished, he could scarcely be – certainly we could not know him to be – perfect love. Thus our hope of immortality is of quite primary importance when regarded both doctrinally and emotionally as a part of, because a necessary consequence of, our faith in God. There is here a stupendous paradox; but it is the paradox which is characteristic of all true religion. We must spiritually renounce all other loves for love of God; yet when we find God, or, rather, when we know ourselves as found of him, we find in and with him all the loves which for his sake we had forgone. If my desire is first for future life for myself, or even first for

5

reunion with those whom I have loved and lost, then the doctrine of immortality may do me positive harm by fixing me in that self-concern or concern for my own joy in my friends. But if my desire is first for God's glory and for myself that I may be used to promote it, then the doctrine of immortality will give me new heart in the assurance that what here must be a very imperfect service may be made perfect hereafter, that my love of friends may be one more manifestation of the overflowing Love Divine, and that God may be seen as perfect Love in the eternal fellowship of love to which he calls us.

For these reasons it seems to me, so far as I can judge, positively undesirable that there should be experimental proof of our survival of death – at least of such survival in the case of those who have had no spiritual faith on earth. For this would bring the hope of immortality into the area of purely intellectual apprehension. It might or might not encourage the belief that God exists; it would certainly, as I think, make very much harder the essential business of faith, which is the transference of the centre of interest and concern from self to God. If such knowledge comes, it must be accepted, and we must try to use it for good and not for evil. And I could never urge the cessation of inquiry in any direction; I cannot ask that so-called psychical research should cease. But I confess I hope that such research will continue to issue in such dubious results as are all that I can trace to it up to date.

When we turn from the relation of this doctrine to religion and consider its relation to ethics we are confronted with a different but, as it were, parallel paradox. The expectation of rewards and punishments in a future life has certainly played a considerable part in disciplining the wayward wills of men. And of this as of other discipline it is true that there may grow up under it a habit of mind which afterwards persists independently of it. But so far as conduct is governed by hope of rewards or fear of punishments as commonly understood, it is less than fully moral. We are probably

agreed in rejecting the extreme austerity of the Kantian doctrine that the presence of pleasure in association with an
action is enough to destroy its moral character; but even
more probably we shall agree that if an act is done for the
sake of resultant pleasure or profit, so that apart from that
pleasure or profit it would not be done, it is not a truly moral
act. Consequently the ethical utility of heaven and hell, conceived as reward and punishment, is disciplinary and preparatory only. So far as true moral character is established,
whether with or without their aid in the process, it becomes
independent of their support and will only be injured by
reference to them.

Moreover, the utility of hell, so conceived, is very early
exhausted, even if it be not from the outset overweighted by
disadvantages. For in ethics as in religion the fundamental
aim is to remove self from the centre of interest and concern.
But fear is the most completely self-centred of all emotions,
and to curb irregularity of conduct by constant use of fear
may easily make this aim harder of attainment than it was
at the outset. I think it is good for most people to have an
occasional shock of fright with reference to their short-
comings; there is no doubt that to live under the constant
pressure of fear – in the sense of anxiety concerning one's
self – is deeply demoralizing.

It is notorious that Kant, while excluding hope of profit
from the motives of a truly moral act, yet found himself
bound to postulate immortality as a means of securing that
adjustment of goodness and happiness which he considered
reason to demand. I believe this line of argument to be sub-
stantially sound. But if it is, then we find that the hope of
immortality is wholesome as an implicate in an independently established morality, though if introduced earlier it
may hinder as much as help that establishment of morality,
just as it has high value as an implicate in faith in God,
though if introduced earlier it may hinder as much as help
the establishment of such faith.

7

All that has so far been said is introductory to our positive reconstruction, and has aimed rather at clearing the ground. We shall find that the authentic Christian doctrine of the future life is free from the objections which lie against the general notion of immortality, while it contains all which in that notion is of religious value or of ethical utility. This Christian doctrine has three special characteristics:

(a) It is a doctrine, not of immortality, but of resurrection.
(b) It regards this resurrection as an act and gift of God, not an inherent right of the human soul as such.
(c) It is not a doctrine of rewards and punishments, but is the proclamation of the inherent joy of love and the inherent misery of selfishness.

(a) The Christian doctrine is a doctrine not of immortality but of resurrection. The difference is profound. The method of all non-Christian systems is to seek an escape from the evils and misery of life. Christianity accepts them at their worst, and makes them the material of its triumphant joy. That is the special significance in this connexion of the Cross and Resurrection of Jesus Christ. Stoics teach an indifference to death; the Gospel teaches victory over it. Richard Lewis Nettleship said our aim should be to reach a frame of mind in which we should pass through the episode of physical death without being so much as aware of it. That is a splendid utterance; and yet it implies a detachment from wholesome interests and from the intercourse of friends which is a little inhuman. Surely it is true that death is a fearful calamity – in itself; and as such the Gospel accepts it; there is no minimizing of its terrors. Only its sting – its very real sting – is drawn; only its victory – its very real victory – is converted into the triumph of its victim. It is one thing to say that there is no real tragedy in the normal course of human life; it is quite another thing to acknowledge the tragedy and then to claim that it is transformed into glory.

We lose very much if we equate this hope of transformation, of resurrection whole and entire in all that may pertain to fullness of life, into a new order of being, with a doctrine of mere survival. Incidentally, though the theme is too great to be developed here, this glorious Christian hope coheres with a totally different conception of the relation of time or history to eternity; for it both clothes history with an eternal significance, and at the same time points to a conception of eternity as something much more than the totality of time; and time becomes not so much the 'moving image of eternity' as a subordinate and essentially preparatory moment in the eternal reality. But that fascinating and bewildering topic would require a whole lecture to itself.

(*b*) The Christian conception of the life to come as a gift of God has affinities with the Platonic doctrine of immortality. Plato had sought to demonstrate the inherent immortality of the individual soul. In the *Phaedo* he fashioned an argument which seems for the moment to have satisfied him. But in fact it is invalid. What Plato proves in the *Phaedo* is that the soul cannot both be, and be dead; he does not prove that it cannot pass out of existence altogether. In the *Republic* he advances an argument of which the minor premise seems to be simply untrue. He says that what perishes does so by its own defeat; but the essential disease of the soul – injustice – does not cause, or tend towards, the decay of the soul; therefore the soul is imperishable. But there is every reason to deny the second proposition. When once the essential nature of the soul as self-motion is established, it is at least open to question whether injustice is not a negation of that quality. No doubt the wicked man may display great activity; so may metal filings in the proximity of a magnet; that does not mean that they are endowed with self-motion.

It is in the *Phaedrus* that Plato first reaches the clear conception of the soul as characterized essentially by self-motion, and argues from this its indestructibility. But not each individual soul is completely self-moved, and the argument, supposing it to be valid, as I think it is, only establishes the indestructibility of the spiritual principle in the universe, not the immortality of each individual soul. Plato seems to have accepted that result, for in the *Laws*, where we find his final conclusions, he declares that only God is immortal in his own right, and that he of his bounty bestows on individual souls an immortality which is not theirs by nature.

That this is the prevailing doctrine of the New Testament seems to me beyond question as soon as we approach its books free from the Hellenistic assumption that each soul is inherently immortal in virtue of its nature as soul. That is a view which is increasingly hard to reconcile with psychology. But psychology is still a nascent science and cannot as yet claim any great degree of deference. I do not claim that in the New Testament there is a single doctrine everywhere accepted; on the contrary it seems to me that here and there a relapse into the Hellenistic point of view may be detected. But its prevailing doctrine, as I think, is that God alone is immortal, being in his own nature eternal; and that he offers immortality to men not universally but conditionally. Certainly we come very near to a direct assertion of the first part of this position in the description of God as 'the blessed and only Potentate, the King of them that reign as kings, and Lord of them that rule as lords, who only hath immortality' (1 Tim. 6.16). The only approach to an argument for a future life of which our Lord makes use is based on the relationship of God to the soul: 'He is not the God of the dead, but of the living: for all live unto Him' (Luke 20.38). And in close connexion with this saying in the Lucan version are the words, 'they that are accounted worthy to attain to that world and the resurrection from the dead' (Luke 20.35). It is in consonance with this that the Resurrection of Jesus Christ is constantly spoken of throughout the New Testament as the act of God himself. No doubt St Paul explicitly states that 'We must all be made manifest before the judgment seat of Christ' (2 Cor. 5.10) but that settles nothing, unless we make, with some followers of 'psychical research', the entirely unwarrantable assumption that the survival of physical death is the same thing as immortality. Quite clearly it is not; for a man might survive the death of his body only to enter then upon a process of slow or rapid annihilation. And St Paul elsewhere declares that he follows the Christian scale of values 'if that by any means I might attain to the resurrection of the dead' (Phil. 3.1).

Are there not, however, many passages which speak of the endless torment of the lost? No; as far as my knowledge goes there is none at all. There are sayings which speak of being cast into undying fire. But if we do not approach these with the pre-supposition that what is thus cast in is indestructible, we shall get the impression, not that it will burn for ever, but that it will be destroyed. And so far as the difficulty is connected with the terms 'eternal' or 'everlasting', as in Matt. 26.46 ('eternal punishment') it must be remembered that the Greek word used is αἰώνιος which has primary reference to the quality of the age to come and not to its infinity. The word that strictly means 'eternal' is not frequent in the New Testament, but it does occur, so that we must not treat the commoner word as though it alone had been available, and when a vital issue turns on the distinction it is fair to lay some stress upon it. And after all, annihilation is an everlasting punishment though it is not unending torment.

But the stress in the New Testament is all laid upon the quality of the life to come and the conditions of inheriting eternal life. It is not to a mere survival of death that we are called, while we remain very much what we were before; it is to a resurrection to a new order of being, of which the chief characteristic is fellowship with God. Consequently the quality of the life to which we are called is determined by the Christian doctrine of God.

What is abundantly clear throughout the New Testament is its solemn insistence upon what Baron von Hügel spoke of as 'abiding consequences'. Language is strained and all the imagery of apocalypse employed to enforce the truth that a child's choice between right and wrong matters more than the courses of the stars. Whatever is done bears fruit for ever; whatever a man does, to all eternity he is the man who did that. Moreover, evil-doing entails for the evil-doer calamity hereafter if not also here, while for him who gives himself to the will of God there is stored up joy unspeakable.

Further, there can be no question that our Lord was prepared to use a certain appeal to self-interest to re-inforce the claims of righteousness: 'It is good for thee to enter into life with one eye rather than having two eyes to be cast into the hell of fire' (Matt. 17.8). But these passages are mostly connected with cases where loyalty to righteousness involves some great sacrifice or self-mortification; they are not so much direct appeals to self-interest as counter-weights to the self-interest that might hinder the sacrifice or mortification required. And the positive invitation to discipleship is never based on self-interest. He never says, 'If any man will come after me, I will deliver him from the pains of hell and give him the joys of heaven'. He calls men to take up their cross and share his sacrifice. To those who are weary and heavy laden there is the promise of rest; but the general invitation is to heroic enterprise involving readiness for the completest self-sacrifice, and concern for the mere saving of the soul is condemned as a sure way of losing it.

We are called to fellowship with Christ, in whom we see the eternal God. It is fellowship with Love, complete and perfect in its self-giving. How weak is the lure which this offers to our selfish instincts! There is in the Gospel a warning that the way of self-will leads to destruction, so that prudence itself counsels avoidance of it. But when we turn to seek another way there is none that commends itself to prudence only. For the reward that is offered is one that a selfish man would not enjoy. Heaven, which is fellowship with God, is only joy for those to whom love is the supreme treasure. Indeed, objectively regarded, heaven and hell may well be

identical. Each is the realization that Man is utterly subject
to the purpose of another – of God who is Love. To the godly
and unselfish soul that is joy unspeakable; to the selfish soul
it is a misery against which he rebels in vain. Heaven and
hell are the two extreme terms of our possible reactions to
the Gospel of the Love of God. 'This is the judgment, that
the light is come into the world, and men loved the darkness
rather than the light' (John 3.19). 'This is life eternal, that
they should know thee the only true God, and him whom
thou didst send, even Jesus Christ' (John 17.3).

If with such thoughts to guide us, and paying regard to
what seems the best help that contemporary thought can give
us, we try in any way to schematize our beliefs in the future
life, I suggest that the result is somewhat as follows.

God has created us as children of his love, able to understand that love in some degree and to respond to it. In the
psycho-physical organism of human personality there is the
possibility for a development of the spiritual elements, in response to and communion with the eternal God, which
makes these capable of receiving from God the gift of his own
immortality. Unless there has been such degeneration that
only animal life continues to exist, it must be presumed that
this possibility remains; and as it is hardly conceivable that
any human being descends altogether to the level of the animal during this mortal life, it is further to be presumed that
every personality survives bodily death. But that is not the
same as to attain to immortality. And here we are confronted
with a dilemma, which I expect will remain insoluble so long
as we have available only those data which are afforded by
experience on this side of death. On the one hand is the
supreme significance of human freedom, which seems to involve the possibility for every soul that it may utterly and
finally reject the love of God; and this must involve it in
perdition. God must assuredly abolish sin; and if the sinner
so sinks himself in his sin as to become truly identified with
it, God must destroy him also. On the other hand this result

13

is failure on the part of God; for though he asserts his supremacy by destruction of the wicked, yet such victory is in fact defeat. For he has no pleasure in the death of him that dieth. The love which expressed itself in our creation can find no satisfaction in our annihilation, and we are prompted by faith in God's almighty love to believe, not in the total destruction of the wicked, but rather in some

> sad obscure sequestered state
> Where God unmakes but to re-make the soul
> He else first made in vain; which must not be.

As I have said, I do not think the dilemma can be resolved by us here on earth. At one time I confess that I was almost confident in accepting Universalism. Later I began to waver, and was much interested, when I told von Hügel that I was moving away from Universalism, to receive his reply that he found himself moving towards it. But while I am now by no means confident, I will offer what slender hope of a solution to the difficulty I am able to entertain.

There is one condition on which our conduct can be both free and externally determined. It is found wherever a man acts in a certain way in order to give pleasure to one whom he loves. Such acts are free in the fullest degree; yet their content is wholly determined by the pleasure of the person loved. Above all do we feel free when our love goes out in answer to love shewn to us. Now the Grace of God is his love made known and active upon and within us; and our response to it is both entirely free and entirely due to the activity of his love towards us. All that we could contribute of our own would be the resistance of our self-will. It is just this which love breaks down, and in so doing does not override our freedom but rather calls it into exercise. There is, therefore, no necessary contradiction in principle between asserting the full measure of human freedom and believing that in the end the Grace of God will win its way with every human heart.

But this must be interpreted in the light of the doctrine of 'abiding consequences'. If I allow myself to become set in self-centredness the love of God can only reach me through pain; and when it has found me and stirred my penitence and won me to forgiveness, I am still the forgiven sinner, not the always loyal child of God. And this general truth has application to every act of moral choice.

Again, because God is Love, the universe is so ordered that self-seeking issues in calamity. Thus we are warned that even when judged from its own standpoint self-seeking is unprofitable. But while mercy in this way gives to selfishness the only warning it is capable of heeding, there is no way offered of avoiding the calamity while the selfishness remains. The fear of future pain or of destruction may stimulate a man for his own self's sake to seek salvation; but the only salvation that exists or can exist is one that he can never find while he seeks it for his own self's sake. The warning is a warning that while he remains the sort of man he is, there is no hope for him; it is a call, not merely to a grudging change of conduct for fear of worse or hope of better; it is a call to a change of heart which can only exist so far as it is not grudging but willing. Thus it is a call for surrender to that Grace of God which alone can effect such a change of heart. It is Love that keeps aflame the hell of fire to warn us that in selfishness there is no satisfaction even for self; and Love then calls the soul which heeds that warning to submit itself to the moulding influences of Love by which it may be transformed; and the promise is of a joy which only those who are transformed into the likeness of Love can know, while to others it is the very misery from which they seek deliverance.

In such a view there is neither the demoralizing influence of a cheery optimism which says, 'Never mind; it will all come right in the end', nor the equally demoralizing influence of a terrorism which stereotypes self-centredness by undue excitation of fear. There is an appeal to self-concern in those who can heed no other, but it is an appeal to leave all self-concern behind. Again there is no promise for the future which can encourage any soul to become forgetful of God, for the promise is of fellowship with God, and therein, but only therein, of fellowship also with those whom we have loved. It is an austere doctrine, more full of the exigency than of the consolations of religion, though it offers these also in gracious abundance to all who submit to its demands, for to be drawn into fellowship with God is to find that the communion of saints is a reality. And the core of the doctrine is this: Man is not immortal by nature or of right; but there is offered to him resurrection from the dead and life eternal if he will receive it from God and on God's terms. There is nothing arbitrary in that offer or in those terms, for God is perfect Wisdom and perfect Love. But Man, the creature and helpless sinner, cannot attain to eternal life unless he gives himself to God, the Creator, Redeemer, Sanctifier, and receive from him both worthiness for life eternal and with that worthiness eternal life.

Rebirth or Immortality?

SYDNEY CAVE

There can be few aspects of the Christian doctrine of immortality which have not been discussed and defended by previous lecturers on the Drew foundation. But the Christian doctrine of immortality is not the only solution offered of the problem of the life to come. There is another solution: the doctrine of transmigration and rebirth. It is a doctrine which has not lacked admirers in modern Europe. Goethe used it to explain the attraction he felt in one of the ladies whom he loved. In some previous existence she had surely been his wife. Thinkers like David Hume and Schopenhauer have spoken of this doctrine of rebirth as the only form of belief in an after-life worthy of a philosopher's attention, whilst, in our own days, a philosopher so eminent as Dr McTaggart speaks of the possibility of rebirth in words of almost lyric beauty. But in the West the doctrine has an exotic air. It is an ingenious surmise, a great perhaps. It expresses the speculation of the few; it is not the conviction of the masses of the people. Only in the East is it a life-axiom, and my excuse for venturing to speak on it is, that for some years I lived in almost daily contact with men to whom it was the logical *prius* of all their thought and the sure explanation of life's tragedies and inequalities.

I

The origin of this doctrine of transmigration and *karma* is still obscure. It is altogether alien from the simple piety of the *Rigveda*. There life was prized, and men prayed that they might 'live a hundred lengthened autumns',[1] and trusted that, when at last death came, they might enjoy in the world

17

to come a life, like that on earth, but more rich and joyous. Even in the dreary period of the *Brāhmaṇas* it was still life, not death, men sought, and by now there was the fear of death, not in this life alone, but in the life to come. And with this dread of future death, we find traces of a hope of future birth which might lead again to life on earth, for rebirth is as yet regarded, not as curse, but boon.[2] Already we find the beginnings of that belief in the retributive adaptation of circumstance and conduct which the doctrine of *karma* was later to express; for, in a difficult passage, it is taught that a man is born into the world which he has made.[3] But such references are few, and seem to be little more than stray surmises. First, in the *Upanishads* do we find the clear formulation of that doctrine of transmigration and of *karma* which became the distinctive feature of Indian thought, and, through the spread of Buddhism, was carried far and wide into Asiatic lands.

It is probable that the earliest reference to the doctrine in the *Upanishads* is to be found in an obscure speech by Yājñavalkya, the great Brāhman sage. Yājñavalkya had claimed a prize offered by a king to the wisest Brāhman, and when his right to this was challenged by Ārtabhāga, justified his claim by revealing the way of knowledge by which the sage might gain the endless world. Ārtabhāga then asked about the man not thus redeemed, but this Yājñavalkya would not answer before others. 'We two only will know of this. This is not for us two to speak of in public. The two went away and deliberated. What they said was *karma* (action). What they praised was *karma*. Verily, one becomes good by good action, bad by bad action.'[4] In the same *Upanishad*, Yājñavalkya expounds his new-found secret in metaphors which have become the commonplaces of Indian thought. The soul passes from body to body, like a caterpillar passing from leaf to leaf, and makes for itself new embodiments like a goldsmith remodelling a piece of gold. 'The doer of good becomes good. The doer of evil becomes evil.' 'As is his desire, such is his resolve; as is his resolve, such the action he performs; what action he performs, that he procures for himself.'[5]

The doctrine, thus isolated, is plain and intelligible. A man's acts create his destiny, and the soul wins for itself in its next birth an embodiment which corresponds to its acts in this. But in a country as conservative as India, the old is rarely displaced entirely by the new, and this new and mysterious doctrine of soul-wandering was combined with the early eschatology which spoke of the world where Yama, the first man, ruled over the spirits of the blessed. Men went there by the *Way of the Fathers*. From it the evil were shut out. For them there was only the lower darkness. A higher way there was, the *Way of the Gods*, by which Agni bore the sacrificial offerings to the gods, and, by that way also, men might ascend to enjoy the bliss of the gods. The classic texts for the doctrine of transmigration and *karma* incorporate with this doctrine these earlier views. In India, where cremation is common, it was natural to think of the burning of the dead as a sacrifice borne upwards to the gods by Agni, the god of the sacrificial fire, and these texts teach first the obscure doctrine of the five fires. The faith of the dead man passes upwards, and is five times offered in sacrifice to the gods, and in these five fires is depicted the stages of the soul's descent to be reborn on earth. From the moon, the soul passes into rain; from rain, into food; from food, into the seed of the male, and from this is formed the embryo from which, in due time, appears the man. With this doctrine is combined the doctrine of the two paths. The wise, who know the doctrine of the five fires, 'and those, too, who in the forest truly worship faith', ascend by the bright Way of the Gods to the worlds of Brahman and for them 'there is no return'. Men, devout and good, but unillumined thus, ascend by the less splendid Way of the Fathers to the moon, and from there descend, in the way described, to be born again on earth. In the *Bṛihadāraṇyaka Upanishad* there is a third path. 'Those who know not these two ways, become crawling and flying insects, and whatever there is here that bites.'[6]

The doctrine of transmigration and *karma*, so expressed, is very hard to visualize, and the passage of the soul from rain into seed seems a precarious one; but the main idea is clear. The wise pass up by the Way of the Gods to the world of Brahman, from which there is no return. The devout pass by the Way of the Fathers to the moon, and, after enjoying there the fruit of their good works, are born again on earth. The careless are, after death, born on earth as noxious insects. In the corresponding passage in the *Chhāndogya Upanishad* a differentiation is made among those who journey along the Way of the Fathers to the moon. Those of 'pleasant conduct' here will obtain a 'pleasant birth' in one of the high castes. Those of repulsive conduct will have a repulsive birth, be born as dog, or swine, or outcaste.[7] As retribution is thus active in the Way of the Fathers, there is no need for the third path, mentioned in the *Bṛihadāraṇyaka Upanishad*, yet this too is retained, and this confusing addition has become an integral part of later Indian thought. Such are the classic texts for the Hindu doctrine of transmigration and *karma*. Their inconsistencies are manifest, and in the *Upanishads* themselves the attempt is made to reconcile them. Thus in the *Kaushītaki Upanishad* it is taught that all who depart from this world go to the moon. Only later do the two paths diverge, so that those unfit to dwell there descend as rain, and are born 'either as a worm, or a moth, or as a fish, or as a bird, or as a lion, or as a wild boar, or as a snake, or as a tiger, or as a person, or as some other in this or that condition, he is born again here according to his deeds (*karman*), according to his knowledge'.[8]

The *Upanishads* are not systematic works. They give the utterances, not of philosophers, but of seers, and it would be unreasonable to expect to find in them clear and coherent teaching. But the inconsistencies of the doctrine of transmigration and *karma* seem to be more than accidental. Cer-

20

tainly they are in no way removed in the elaborate exposition
of the Vedānta given by Śaṅkarāchārya, who ranks among
the greatest systematizers of our race. Esoterically he holds
that nothing is real but the attributeless Brahman. Exoteric-
ally, there is the karmic order in which gods and men are
alike involved. He was evidently acutely conscious of the difficulties of the doctrine of transmigration. What connexion,
for instance, is there between the soul in this birth and the
next? To this, his answer is hesitating and confused, whilst
to the question, why should souls be reborn, 'when they
ascend to the sphere of the moon for the express purpose of
finding there a complete requital of their works', he gives
an answer more curious than convincing. 'When only a little
of the effects of their works is left, they can no longer stay
there. For, as some courtier, who has joined the king's court
with all the requisites which the king's service demands, is
unable to remain at court any longer when, in consequence
of his long stay most of his things are worn out, so that he
is perhaps left with a pair of shoes and an umbrella only;
so the soul, when possessing only a small particle of the effects
of its works, can no longer remain in the sphere of the moon.'[9]
But Śaṅkarāchārya seems to feel himself the inadequacy of
this explanation and suggests that a solution may be found in
the difference between ritual and moral works. Ritual works
earn heaven; failure to perform them, hell. Moral works earn
on earth an appropriate birth. Thus the greatest of crimes,
such as the murder of a Brāhman, require many evil births
on earth to expiate them.[10] Śaṅkarāchārya's suggestion does
not seem to have had much influence, and popular literature
depicts with lurid detail the frightful hells and the loathsome
births on earth which alike await the doer of evil deeds.

II

Difficult as is the doctrine of transmigration and *karma*,
obscure and inconsistent as is its presentation in the classic
Hindu texts, it has become the logical *prius* of Hindu thought.

I think we can all feel its attractiveness. As a recent writer
remarks, 'There is an undeniable dignity in the Hindu conception of the soul, pursuing its long pilgrimage through
decaying worlds, until at length it reaches home in the endless sea.'[11] To Hindus themselves, the interest of the doctrine
is not so much speculative as practical. They are not greatly
concerned with forecasts of future births, or with attempts
to remember past existences. What they are concerned to
have is this: an explanation of life's inequalities. And in the
doctrine of *karma* they rightly claim to have an explanation
which all alike can understand and which does seem to vindicate the justice of the universe.

Any explanation is easier to defend than no explanation,
and that is where Hinduism seems to have the advantage
over Christianity. Soon after I went to India, first the
nephew, and then the son of an honoured Indian colleague
died of typhoid, just as they were completing very successful
university careers. A Hindu judge, who was calling on me
a few days after the second death, asked me how I explained
it all. I had no explanation, but he had. It was due to some
evil *karma* of the past. Yet such explanations, facile as they
are, do not make life's burdens easier to carry. It is all very
well for the Brāhman to ascribe his advantages to the good
karma accumulated in a previous birth, but it does not help
the Pariah to be told that his degradation, which makes his
very proximity a contamination to the Brāhman, is due to
evil deeds, done in an earlier life of which he has no knowledge and no recollection. For the miserable it is no gospel
to be told that 'the Good Law is working on with undeviating
accuracy, that its Agents apply it everywhere with unerring
insight, with unfailing strength, and that all is therefore very
well with the world and with its struggling Souls'.[12] Actually
the universal Hindu view has been that all is not 'very well
with the world and its struggling souls'. The world is getting
steadily and inevitably worse. The golden age was in the
past. Ours is the *kali yuga*, the iron age, last and most evil

22

of all. Nor for those who find life an ill, is there the consolation of life's transiency. A Western poet can sing:

> This life holds nothing good for us;
> But it ends soon, and never more can be;
> But we know nothing of it ere our birth,
> And can know nothing when consigned to earth,
> I ponder these thoughts, and they comfort me.

'This life holds nothing good for us.' That, in all the later *Upanishads*, was held to be an obvious truth. But life recurs and recurs, and escape from the bondage of rebirth became the supreme quest of Indian thought.

The doctrine has not only increased the misery it professes to explain. It has led to an undue acquiescence in others' sorrows. The blind, the maimed, the downtrodden and the bereaved are not unfortunates to be helped and comforted; they are criminals enduring the inexorable consequences of evil deeds. And this has stayed the course of pity, and allowed harsh customs to remain unchecked. Thus, when Christian missionaries began their work among the outcastes, they were told by Hindus that the work would be in vain. The degradation and semi-servitude of the outcastes were the inevitable results of deeds done in a previous birth which in this lifetime have to be expiated. The Hindu doctrine has been proved false to fact. There are in South India many Christians of outcaste origin who, in education and character, are at least the equal of many high caste Hindus. The success of these movements deserves more attention than it has generally received, for it is clear proof that a man's lot is not the fixed result of deeds done in a previous birth. Spiritual forces can, in an improved environment, produce even in his present life a radical change of a man's character and circumstances. Today, in imitation of the Christian Church, there are Hindu societies for the uplift of the depressed classes. It is significant of much that the most ardent workers have belonged, not to orthodox Hinduism, but to the

23

Prārthanā Samàj, in which the doctrine of *karma* is rejected or ignored. Yet this is surely natural. It is hard to work for the unfortunate, if we regard them, not as unfortunate, but accursed, incapable in this life of any improvement.

The doctrine of transmigration and *karma*, though primarily an attempt to explain life's inequalities, is also an assertion of the principle of retribution. Here too its success seems incomplete. There is an apparent poetic justice in the popular form of the doctrine. As the *Laws of Manu* put it, 'Men who delight in doing hurt become carnivorous animals; those who eat forbidden food, worms; thieves, creatures who consume their own kind.' 'For stealing grain, a man becomes a rat.' 'For stealing meat, a vulture, for stealing vehicles, a camel.'[13] Against such a form of the theory, Herder's criticism is still unanswerable. If a man, who is a tiger in cruelty, becomes at his next birth an actual tiger, that is no true expiation. As a tiger he will have no conscience, and will be able to ravage and kill without remorse. And in its more subtle forms, the doctrine still fails to reveal the connexion between the joys and sorrows of this life, and the good deeds and bad of a previous existence. It is hard to believe that the newborn babe, in its appealing helplessness and apparent innocence, is really an old and world-weary traveller, who in former births may have been, not innocent, but wicked and sensual. And, when the child grows up, what knowledge has it of any earlier existences? Mr Leadbeater can tell us quite a lot about previous lives. Who of us can make that claim? And, like ourselves, most Hindus confess that they know nothing about their former births. Thus, in the *Bhagavadgītā* Kṛishṇa expressly says that it is by his divine power that he knows of his previous incarnations, whilst Arjuna, his royal worshipper, is ignorant of his. And much of the awe with which men regarded Gautama the Buddha was due to the belief that he had the supernatural power of knowing of his own and others' earlier lives. Nor has Hindu philosophy succeeded in explaining the connexion between the deeds of a former birth and this present existence. We have only to turn to Śaṅkarāchārya's elaborate discussion of this problem to realise the difficulty of relating the effects of past deeds to a soul which is regarded as neutral and insentient.

The doctrine of *karma* in its classic Hindu form makes of retribution an inevitable law, concerned not with doers but with deeds. It is surely not an accident that the *Upanishads* which first formulate this doctrine have as their prime quest a redemption which ignores altogether the effect of deeds. The doctrine of *karma* treats retribution as an end, and not a means. Its justice is more blind and inexorable than that of the most unimaginative and pedantic of our judges, for, crude and harsh as criminal justice often is, judges are expected to take into consideration the degree to which the wrongdoer is responsible. But in the Hindu view, justice works blindly on, and deeds and their effects are thought of as if they were terms in an algebraic equation. And from the time of the *Upanishads*, the supreme endeavour of Hindu thought has been, in natural reaction, to escape altogether from a bondage more terrible than that which any law court can inflict, for it lasts, not for one lifetime, but for an endless succession of births and deaths. And so the redemption which the *Upanishads* proclaim, and which Śaṅkarāchārya and many a philosopher since have reaffirmed, is a redemption unrelated in any way to deeds, a redemption which comes from the intuitive realization of the unity of the soul with Brahman. For redemption, thus conceived, good deeds are, at best, only a preliminary. As the *Upanishads* sometimes assert with almost brutal emphasis, for the man thus redeemed, good and evil deeds alike have no meaning, for all activity belongs to that illusory sphere from which the wise man is liberated. And that is part of the tragedy of Indian life today. The doctrine of *karma*, by its exclusive emphasis on retribution, has led to a view of redemption which empties life in the world of meaning, a redemption whose nearest analogy is a dreamless sleep. Such a redemption is no Gospel for a rejuvenated India. Nor are Hindus today content to regard this age as a *kali yuga*, an iron age, and to look backwards to a golden past. Many of them are looking forward with high hopes to the time when India shall have a great and honoured place in the councils of the world. They desire to break down the barriers of caste, to uplift the depressed, and to unite all Indians in proud service to their Motherland, but the doctrine of *karma* is a grave obstacle. It unnerves effort, for it turns the unfortunate into the accursed, and makes this present life incapable of improvement, for each man's life is the inexorable effect of deeds done in previous lives of which he has no knowledge.

III

It would appear then that the doctrine of *karma* has increased the burden of the sorrow it sought to explain, and, by over-emphasizing retribution, has led to a view of redemption which ignores altogether the effect of deeds. Yet the doctrine does provide an explanation of life's injustices which all can understand, and, if it be a mere contest of rival theories, it would be hard to show that this doctrine should be abandoned in favour of that doctrine of natural immortality which has been common in the West. In the East, men have seen in existence mere evil, and found in the annihilation of personality the supreme redemption. In the West, it has been commoner to desire the continuity of existence and to regard annihilation as, at most, a dreadful possibility reserved for the finally impenitent. Apart from a belief in God, I do not know that the view of the West has much advantage over that of the East. Why should men desire life after death, if they have no interests which reach beyond the grave, why regard immortality as a boon, if the things they prize are not such as have eternal value? Dealt with in isolation, the two theories are both best regarded as reasonable, but precarious hypotheses. The issue between them cannot be settled by general considerations. It can be settled, if at all, only by reference to our faith in God.

It is here that we have the contrast between the Hindu and the Christian view. The forerunners of Christ, the great Hebrew prophets, ignored altogether the current beliefs in the existence of the spirits of the dead. Sheol was a half-pagan idea, for it was generally regarded as a sphere in which the souls of the dead were cut off from the presence of God. Only after men had realized what a true communion with God might be, did they conceive of an immortality which meant, not the dim existence of a material soul, but the perpetuation of a communion with God begun on earth. I doubt myself if there be any other way by which assurance of the Christian doctrine of immortality can be secured. God is the God, not of the dead, but of the living. He is a God who will not allow the communion men have had with him to lapse by death. These words of Jesus are worth more for the Christian doctrine of immortality than many an elaborate argument. Communion with such a God as he revealed must be eternal. The Father of our Lord and Saviour Jesus Christ is a God who, having loved, loves to the end.

We are concerned then in Christianity, not with a belief in natural immortality to which our belief in God has to be adjusted, but with faith in the God whom Christ revealed, of which the belief in immortality is the inevitable correlate. It is here that the real issue between Hinduism and Christianity lies. In Hinduism the belief in *karma* is fundamental, and it has been found impossible to combine with this, belief in a God who is both ultimately real and personally active. The karmic order is inexorable. Every deed creates its effect. If God were active, he too would be bound by the karmic order, and so Hindu speculation, in its most influential form, has taught that the one reality is the Brahman who is insentient and attributeless. In his exposition of one of Bādarāyaṇa's *Sutras*, Śaṅkarāchārya expressly states that the creation of the world was without aim or purpose.[14] Īsvara, the creator, is but the highest of the effected gods, under *karma*, and so unreal with the unreality of the whole karmic process. Even Rāmānuja's valiant attempt to legitimatize in the Vedānta a more theistic faith breaks down here. At times he speaks of the supreme Brahman as at once personal and real, yet in his discussion of this *Sūtra* of Bādarāyaṇa he has no better solution than Śaṅkarāchārya gave. The highest Brahman made, or rather 'arranged', the world in motiveless sport, and Rāmānuja evidently believed that, if God had motive or desire, he too would fall under the karmic law.

A meaningless reality, or a living God who is unreal: it is a harsh alternative, and one that Indian devotion has often tried to evade.

Probably it is to this endeavour that the most prized today of all Hindu books, the *Bhagavadgītā*, owes much of its popularity. In it Kṛishṇa is proclaimed as a living God, personal and supreme, who loves men and seeks the good of those that worship him. Yet, though active, he is free from the karmic law, for, though he works, 'works defile him not. He has no longing for the fruit of works.' And in words which have brought comfort to many, he bids his worshipper 'Have thy mind on me, thy devotion toward me, thy sacrifice to me, do homage to me. To me thou shalt come. I make thee a truthful promise; thou art very dear to me. Surrendering all the laws, come for refuge to me alone. I will deliver thee from all sins; grieve not.'[15] Such words as these explain in part the fascination of the book for many an educated Hindu today. Yet even here a true Theism is not reached, and the Kṛishṇa who loves men and seeks their love, is declared to be veiled by illusion and known to none; 'indifferent to all born beings', there is none whom he loves.[16]

The belief in *karma*, which has compelled Indian thinkers to exclude the supreme God from all activity, lest he too be involved in the cycle of deeds and their effects, has only partly affected popular practice. The timorous still have thought it wise to buy off the hostility of evil powers, whilst the devout have prayed to the gods, and asked their help, as if these gods were at once active and real. It is hard to reconcile with the belief in *karma* the intense devotion to the gods which finds expression in much of the vernacular literature. Who, for instance, in reading the *Rāmāyaṇa* of Tulsī Dās would imagine that to its author Rāma was unreal with the unreality of the whole karmic order? It is a personal God that is sought and loved, and the worshipper thinks of him as real and loving. Tulsī Dās himself tells us of one who asked a famous sage to tell him about God, and the great seer began to describe Brahman, in the terms familiar in Hindu thought, as the 'unwishful, the nameless, the formless', identical with the soul of men, but the man replied, 'The worship of the impersonal laid no hold of my heart.'[17] That is surely a true complaint; it is the personal and the known that the heart desires. And with some of these saints, devotion to their God is so intense that their love for him seems to give them at times all that they desire. Thus in Tukārām we find a joy in God so great that he can even turn away from the thought of liberation from the bondage of *karma*, and prefer, to absorption in the Infinite, a rebirth on earth; all earth's sorrows are worth while, if only God be near to help.

> Hear, O God, my supplication—
> Do not grant me Liberation.
>
> 'Tis what men so much desire;
> Yet how much this joy is higher.
>
> Heavenly joy is not for me,
> For it passeth speedily.
>
> But that name how strangely dear,
> That in songs of praise we hear.
>
> Ah, says Tukā, it is this
> Makes our lives so full of bliss.[18]

29

Yet heart and head remain in opposition. The devotion of the *bhakta* and the wisdom of the seer are incompatible. Even where, as in the Śaiva Siddhānta of South India, the most strenuous endeavour is made to reconcile the two, a true Theism is not reached.[19] And this is inevitable, for the inexorable working of the karmic law leaves no room for a living God, active in men's salvation, and ultimately real.

IV

Rebirth or immortality, which of these great historic answers best solves the problem of the life to come? Many today in Europe find very attractive the Eastern answer of rebirth. Some accept it because it seems to explain the obvious inequalities of gifts and circumstances; others are inclined to it, because in their natural revolt against what they think the orthodox doctrine, they are ready to embrace any theory which gives a further probation for that great majority of people who at death seem still too immature in character to have assigned to them a final destiny of weal or woe; others find it reassuring to those Malthusian fears of over-population which they carry over even to the vast spaces of the universe. It has seemed worth while therefore to give some account of the working out of this doctrine in Hinduism, where it is no stray surmise, or fanciful speculation, but the prime axiom of life, influencing all thought and practice. Actually, as we have seen, the doctrine has not alleviated but increased 'the burthen of the mystery', 'the heavy and the weary weight of all this unintelligible world'. Nor is this doctrine one of probation, as some have supposed, an educative process, appointed by a loving God. The soul has no knowledge of previous births, gains no insight from them. It is the victim of a fixed and automatic law of retribution, so that the miseries of this life are the almost mechanical effects of deeds done in a previous existence with which this present life has no discernible connexion. And this over-emphasis on retribution has led to the principle of retribution

being unduly ignored. The doctrine of *karma*, which makes
of retribution an end and not a means, has had as its correlate a view of redemption which seeks to evade altogether
the effect of deeds, and to cut the supreme God off from
all purposed activity lest he too fall under the inexorable
karmic law.

Some facts there are which show that much which has
been attributed to the working out of *karma* is really due to
heredity or environment. If a man of impure life has a child
born blind, it is surely more just that the man should blame
himself than that he should forget his own misdeeds, and
regard his child as a criminal suffering in this life for sins
of a previous birth; yet, if the issue be simply between the
doctrine of *karma* and the doctrine of man's natural immortality, it is unlikely that it will ever be decided. Like most
ultimate problems, this problem is not to be solved by logic.
Our answer will depend upon our thought of God, and our
thought of God we derive less from reasoning than from the
personal judgement of faith. Members of reform movements,
like the Prārthanā Samāj, which reject or ignore the doctrine
of *karma*, do so, so far as we can judge, not because of its
inherent difficulties, but because they have a faith in a living
God whose love gives life too great a meaning for it to be
interpreted only by the karmic law. And converts from caste
Hinduism become Christian, not because they have first
renounced the doctrine of *karma*, but because, in some way
or other, they have begun to think Christ's thought of God,
and so have learnt to judge of life now, and of life hereafter,
from the standpoint of his Gospel. Men feel the appeal of
Christ's words, they gain from him something of his confidence in God's love, and because of this they know themselves to be liberated from the bondage of the karmic order,
that they may be no longer cogs in a great machine, but the
children of a heavenly Father who is active in their lives and
to whose mercy and faithfulness they can gladly leave the
final issue of their own and others' lives.

In Christianity, the belief of immortality is not primary but derivative. It is one of the consequences of faith in the God whom Christ revealed. Unlike Zoroaster and Muhammad, Christ did not speak much of the life to come, nor base his appeal on hopes of heaven or fears of hell. Instead he proclaimed and revealed a God of love with whom already men might have communion. He showed in time the meaning of eternal life, and called men to share with him in the resources of the Kingdom of God, that unseen and supernal realm to which his followers were already introduced. The God he preached was a God of the living, not of the dead, and those who trust the God of Jesus are sure that, in death, and in the life to come, he still will be their God. God is no longer the utterly unknown. He has the content to us of Christ's character, so that such a one as Paul, in spite of the disappointments and hardships of his life, could speak of himself as being 'in Christ'. The unseen for him was no longer the unrevealed, for he already lived his life in God, the God whom Christ had shown. And with such a faith, the problems which the doctrine of *karma* sought to solve are eased, if not explained. Sorrow loses much of its bitterness and its perplexity. And, though retribution is recognized, it is regarded, not as an end, but as a means, for retribution itself serves the purposes of God's redeeming love. The Cross becomes the symbol of God's rule, the revelation of the way God bears the *karma* of our human sin, and the Cross is meant to be the symbol of our service, for none can shirk the Cross who follow Christ. There is no fixed law of *karma*. Instead we have God redeeming man, and men, thus redeemed, taking part in the world's redemption.

The issue then between the Hindu and the Christian doctrines is not primarily one of logical coherency. It goes deep down to our whole conception of God and man, and of the meaning and opportunities of our human lives. The Hindu doctrine of *karma*, in seeking to explain sorrow, has increased its burden. By its over-emphasis on retribution it has led to a view of redemption which ignores altogether the effect of deeds. And some of its implicates are contradicted by the clear witness of experience. Many in India are dissatisfied with this doctrine. They feel that it has led to an undue acquiescence in social cruelties and mocks their dream of a united Motherland restored to what they deem its pristine glory. But they have nothing to put in its place, and many not unnaturally complain that the followers of Christ are as little liberated from the seen as they have felt themselves to be from the bondage of the karmic law. The Christian Gospel speaks of God as redeeming love, and calls us now to an eternal life which death cannot interrupt but will consummate. A message so strange and glad will be believed as it is not only preached but manifested, and the Church will make credible the Christian doctrine of immortality as it shows forth in act the meaning of that communion with God which through Christ we are meant already to experience.

NOTES

1. *Rigveda*, x. 18.
2. *Śatapatha Brahmana*, i. 5. 3. 14.
3. op. cit. vi. 2. 2. 27.
4. *Brihadāranyaka Upanishad*, iii. 2. 6. 13 (Hume's translation).
5. op. cit. iv. 4. 3–5.
6. op. cit. vi. 2. 16.
7. *Chhāndogya Upanishad*, v. 10. 7.
8. *Kaushītaki Upanishad*, i. 2.
9. *Vedāntasūtras*, iii. 1. 8.
10. op. cit. iii. 1. 9–15
11. J. B. Pratt, *India and Its Faiths*, p. 106.
12. Mrs Besant, *Karma*, p. 50.
13. *Laws of Manu*, xii. 59. 62. 63. 67.
14. On *Vedāntasūtras*, ii. 1. 33.
15. xviii. 65. 66 (Dr Barnett's translation).
16. vii. 25. 26; ix. 29.

17. *Rāmāyaṇa*, vii. 107
18. *Psalms of Marāṭhā Saints*, trs. Nicol Macnicol, p. 83.
19. See Schomerus, *Der Śaiva Siddhānta*, p. 430, or Sydney Cave, *Redemption Hindu and Christian*, p. 136.

The Bible and
Personal Immortality

T. W. MANSON

'And David said to his servants "Is the child dead?" They said, "He is dead". Then David arose from the earth, and washed, and anointed himself, and changed his clothes, and he went into the house of the Lord, and worshipped; he then went to his own house; and when he asked, they set food before him, and he ate. Then his servants said to him, "What is this thing that you have done? You fasted and wept for the child while it was alive; but when the child died you arose and ate food." He said, "While the child was still alive, I fasted and wept, for I said, 'Who knows whether the Lord will be gracious to me, that the child may live?' But now he is dead; why should I fast? Can I bring him back again? I shall go to him, but he will not. return to me."'[1]

'I shall go to him, but he will not return to me.' There you have in a dozen words the ultimate heartbreak of human life. It matters little whether we look upon the dead child, his life ended almost before it has begun; or stand in our vast war cemeteries amid the memorials of men cut down in the prime of their manhood; or watch the slow erosion of the human frame by the flood of years. Always the same question asks itself; when external violence or inner decay has done its work, is there anything left that can say to itself, 'Here I am'? Or is the total truth that the physical constituents that made up the brain and brawn of John Smith have now all entered into other relations, and that episode that we called John Smith is completely finished? Man confronted by the wreckage of what was once his brother most

35

naturally asks himself whether there is any hope either of
reconstitution or, failing that, of the salvage of some essential
part of the dead man. And man in ancient times was unwill-
ing to contemplate the possibility of total extinction. True,
you will find Lucretius saying,

> When we shall be no more, when there shall have come
> the parting of body and soul, by whose union we are made
> one, you may know that nothing at all will be able to
> happen to us, who then will be no more, or stir our feeling;
> no, not if earth shall be mingled with sea, and sea with
> sky.[2]

But this is a minority opinion. Most people look to some kind
of continued existence beyond the grave.

In ancient Egypt 'men looked forward to a happy existence in the Sekhet-hetepet or Fields of Peace, where life was
conceived to be practically a continuation of that known on
earth, but without its miseries'.[3] The Babylonians had a less
alluring picture. For them 'the dead lived in an underground
region, which was called Arâlu. It was ruled over by its own
gods, the chief of whom were Nergal and his consort Allatu.
The region itself was dark and gloomy, and offered an un-
attractive existence. The Babylonians saw no reason to fear
punishment or hope for reward beyond the grave, and had
no thought of a resurrection.'[4] The beliefs held in ancient
Israel have considerable similarity to the Babylonian. The
Hebrew Sheol has much more in common with the Babylonian Arâlu than with the Egyptian Fields of Peace. In
order to understand the old Israelite picture of the condition
of the dead in the other world it is necessary to have some
idea of how the Hebrews thought of a living man in this
world; and here I cannot do better than quote Professor
Aubrey Johnson.[5]

> In Israelite thought man is conceived of, not so much in
> dual fashion as 'body' and 'soul', but synthetically as a

unit of vital power or (in current terminology) a psycho-physical organism ... At death, however, the unity of this whole is broken up; the organism as a centre of vital power is destroyed. Nevertheless, this does not mean a man's complete extinction. For some time at least he may live on as an individual (apart from his possible survival within the social unit) in such scattered elements of his personality as the bones, the blood, and the name. Thus death is to be explained in terms of life. It is a weak and indeed ... the weakest form of life; for it involves a complete scattering of one's vital power ... This conception of death as a weak form of life may also be seen in the fact that man is further pictured as living on, a mere shadow of his former self, in company with the *rephaim* in the underworld of Sheol.

Man alive is a 'unit of vital power': man dead is such a unit that has run down. Sheol is the underground depository of the dead. It is 'the deepest place in the universe, just as heaven is the highest. There is room for many, and he who has got down there never returns':[6] 'I shall go to him, but he will not return to me.' Sheol is 'for the most part, a still and silent "land of forgetfulness", which even at its best is but a pale and gloomy reflection of the world of light and life which is Yahweh's special sphere'.[7] We may perhaps illustrate what is meant by the picture of a dump for worn-out motor-cars. They are there. They still exist: rusty, dirty, and battered. They still exist: only they don't go any more. Sheol is like that, a scrap-heap for worn-out human beings. They have not ceased to exist: they have only ceased to possess vital power in any usable quantity. They are totally and permanently incapacitated. This goes with the fact that any weakness or incapacity during life can be regarded, and is regarded, as a form of death; and recovery from such a weakness can be treated as restoration to life.[8] The underlying conviction in all this way of thinking is that real life is the kind of life that is lived in the world as we know it; that it consists in effort and achievement, in acquisition and enjoyment, in loving one's friend and hating one's enemies, in sharing the common life of the family, the clan, and the nation, in joining in the worship of God. The tedium of Sheol lies in the fact that, while its occupants still exist, they can no longer enjoy life. The implication is that any victory over death must be a restoration of vital power and of the opportunity to exercise it in a world of men and things.

At this point we must pause for a moment to take notice of a view that stands in sharp contrast to all this: I mean the doctrine of the immortality of the soul as put forward and defended by the greatest of the Greek philosophers. This depends on making a sharp distinction between mind and matter, soul and body. Man is essentially a soul attached to, even imprisoned in, a body. That soul is akin to God and, when set free from its bodily prison-house with all its tainted associations, it can achieve its natural divinity or immortality – they come to much the same thing. As Cornford says, 'immortality in this sense is to be sharply distinguished from the mere continuance, in some unseen region, of a life resembling life on earth'.[9] It has to be added that, if we make this distinction – as I think we should – then the Bible, like most of us, is concerned precisely with the continuance somewhere of a life resembling, in essentials, if not in all respects, life on earth. Its presuppositions are much the same as ours: that, on the whole and at its best, life is worth living, and that people are worth preserving. The developed teaching of the Bible could not rest content with the doctrine of Sheol, because, though the people who dwell there continue to exist, their existence is in no sense a life worth living. Nor can it accept the Greek doctrine of immortality as it stands because, whether or not the kind of life offered would be a life worth living, it would not be the whole man that would live it.[10]

In the Old Testament we are allowed to see the old doctrine of Sheol being superseded by the doctrine of the resurrection; and it is possible to follow the main lines of the spiritual progress which made the change inevitable. Broadly speaking, it is the revelation of the righteousness of God through the prophets that makes it necessary to go beyond Sheol. There are, I think, two outstanding moments in this progress; one is marked by the book of Job, the other by the book of Daniel.

In the book of Job we are presented with a major difficulty for faith in a righteous God. The matter can be put in this way. Granted that death reduces all men to the same level with complete disregard of character and achievement in this life; then it follows that if the Judge of all the earth is to do right by individual men and women, he must do it in this life. The rewards of virtue and the punishments of wickedness must come to the persons concerned before death. Afterwards it will be too late; for death puts us beyond the reach of rewards and punishments. But Job is presented to us as a man of exemplary character loaded with ghastly afflictions during his lifetime. His friends draw the only possible inference consistent with the justice of God, namely that his apparent virtue must be a mere façade covering deep-seated and persistent wickedness. Job, who knows his own integrity, cannot accept this way out. Yet how can he maintain his own righteousness without impugning that of God? One way out would be to postpone the rehabilitation of Job to the next life and find the statement of that belief in the famous passage in chapter 19, beginning, 'I know that my redeemer liveth'. I have not time to discuss the verses in detail and must be content to say that the admirable discussion by Professor Sutcliffe[11] seems to me to make it impossible to treat this passage as a statement of belief in the resurrection. I do not think that such a belief is present in the book; and when we take the book as it stands, it appears that the justice of God is to be vindicated and the character of Job cleared of suspicion by his restoration to health, happiness and prosperity *in this life*. But, of course, this is merely to shelve the problem. The story of Job is provided with a happy ending, but there are other Jobs – and we know it – whose lives are not rounded off so neatly. The problem remains; and it is no solution to say that if we all got our deserts none would escape whipping, for that is merely to transfer to this life the ethical indifferentism of Sheol.

The problem remained to be raised in a more acute form than ever before in the middle of the second century before Christ. By that time the Jewish religion had become a clear-cut belief in one God, a belief which excluded any recognition whatsoever of any other deity. Along with this monotheistic faith went the moral obligation to give complete obedience to the commandments of God as set out in the Jewish law, and to have complete trust in God's promises as given in Scripture. In the sixties of the second century BC Judaea formed part of the Seleucid kingdom and the policy of the reigning monarch, Antiochus IV Epiphanes, was to make Greek culture and religion the way of life for all his subjects. The result was the first great clash between Church and State. It split the Jewish people and produced both apostates and martyrs. The issue of God's righteousness was presented in a more acute form than ever before. Was it right that those men and women who had laid down their lives in absolute loyalty to God, and those others who had saved their skins by apostasy should, in the end, share the same fate in the abode of the dead? The question demanded an answer; and only one answer was possible. For if God himself made no difference between loyalty and apostasy, it could mean one of two things: either the difference between loyalty and disloyalty was of no importance – which was unthinkable; or it was important, and God's servants were more aware of its importance than God himself – which was equally unthinkable. Only one possibility remained open: to declare that God would not make Sheol the last word. This declaration is made at the beginning of the twelfth chapter of the book of Daniel.

And at that time shall stand forth Michael, the great
prince, who stands for the sons of thy people. And there
shall be a time of tribulation, such as never was since there
was a nation until that time. And in that time thy people
shall be delivered, all who are found written in the book.
And many of those who sleep in the dust of the earth shall
awake, some to everlasting life, and some to shame and
everlasting contempt.

It is not necessary for our present purpose to give an exact
interpretation of all the details of the pictures nor would time
permit it. The essential thing is that it is being made quite
plain that God's concern with men and women is an ethical
concern which does not cease at death; and equally that men
and women are accountable, and their responsibility is not
wiped out in the grave.

In its first formulation the resurrection of the dead seems
to involve their return from the stark and gloomy underworld of Sheol to the light and warmth of this world, where
they may resume life in its fullness, and take their fill of its
joys and satisfactions. In this connexion it is significant that
in St Matthew's account of the Resurrection of our Lord he
tells that many dead people came out of their graves at the
same time and were seen walking about in Jerusalem.[12] That
shows what was ordinarily understood by the word resurrection. It was, of course, possible to think that the resurrection
would be preceded by a radical transformation of the world,
and that there would be a new heaven and a new earth; but
it was the renewed earth that would be the habitation of
those who rose to life.

These new beliefs were widely accepted in Jewish circles.
The principal dissenting voice was that of the Sadducees,
who were opposed to innovations of any kind and held fast
to the old Hebrew orthodoxy of Sheol, the parity of the dead
there, and the impossibility of release from its dismal con-
fines. On this, as on other points, the Sadducees were the

fundamentalists of Judaism in their day; but I cannot stay to moralize on that interesting fact. The main point to which I would draw attention is that it was on this issue of resurrection that they came into open conflict with our Lord, and so provided the occasion for further elucidation of the doctrine of life after death.

Two passages in the Gospels call for special consideration at this point. The first is the parable of Dives and Lazarus.[13] I cannot but think that this parable is directed against the Sadducees. Dives himself is a typical member of their class and he and his brothers are convinced believers in the common lot of all the inhabitants of Sheol. It is consequently a great shock to him to discover when he arrives that there is no parity there. The kind of justice that obtains beyond the grave is sketched in the broadest outlines, so much so that it might be called rough justice. I suspect, though, that we are not meant to spend a great deal of time working out the precise merits and demerits of the two men and trying to decide whether their fates in the next world correspond exactly with what we should think they deserve. The essence of the matter is that there is an assessment made and that it determines what shall happen to the people concerned. Jesus affirms the Jewish doctrine that men carry their past record with them beyond death and that they are answerable for their own character and conduct. It is men and women who live on after death, not shades or disembodied thinking-machines.

The second passage is the dispute between Jesus and the Sadducees, who put to him the hypothetical case of a woman who, under the regulations concerning Levirate marriage, was the wife of seven brothers in succession. This leads up to the supposedly unanswerable question: In the resurrection, when they rise again, whose wife will she be?[14] The form of this question, and indeed the whole statement of the problem, would suggest that the resurrection under discussion is one in which men and women come back from Sheol to this world to resume their life as it was before death carried them away. It would have been a sufficient answer to the legal quibble in the question to point out that Solomon in his life-time actually had a considerable number of wives simultaneously, and that it would be equally reasonable to ask whose husband he was. Jesus, however, refuses to be involved in mock litigation about the conjugal rights of hypothetical husbands, and instead uses the case to bring out two great positive teachings about the resurrection.

He begins by accusing the Sadducees of ignorance of the Scriptures and the power of God.[15] He then goes on to show what kind of life the dead rise to, and why we must believe that they do rise. First, the kind of life: it is like that of the angels. We should not be in too great a hurry to assume that this means that we are to substitute the Greek doctrine of the immortality of disembodied souls for the doctrine of the resurrection.[16] The Jewish mind – and it was to Jewish minds that our Lord was speaking – thought of angels primarily as personal beings, living in a society, and living to do God's will. The resurrection-life is to be thought of as life of this kind and quality. It will be a shared experience because those who live it will have a common interest, the love and service of God. Elsewhere in the teaching of our Lord he uses the figure of a banquet at which the patriarchs of old and the men and women of a later day sit down together.[17] Again we have to realize that the imagery is not to be taken literally. It is meant to convey to us that the resurrection-life has its full happiness, and that that happiness is found and enjoyed in the company of others. The resurrection-life is the life of a society: it is not lived in solitude.

I venture to think that the caution against pressing metaphorical language too far applies also in the case of the parable of the sheep and goats.[18] It is clear that it means to tell us that men are answerable for their conduct and that they will have to answer. It is not by any means so clear that we should conceive of the fate of the unrighteous as one of everlasting torment.[19] From what we otherwise know of the mind and heart of Jesus it is possible to think of him as contemplating total destruction for the completely incorrigible: I do not find it possible to think of him as willingly accepting and approving the blind and senseless brutality of infinite punishment for finite offences, or, what is worse, the amoral despotism of predestination and election.

Such things as these are incompatible with the concept of God which provides the basis for belief in the resurrection. The argument which our Lord uses in favour of the doctrine makes belief in a resurrection to everlasting torment absurd. To that argument I now turn.

As it stands it is so compressed in statement that at first sight it seems to be a mere verbal quibble. It is only when we consider it carefully that its real profundity and cogency appear. Jesus goes back to the primary revelation which called Israel into existence as the people of God, and made known to them the name and nature of God whom henceforth they were to worship and obey. In the Mosaic account of the origin and constitution of Israel, at the point where God spoke to him from the burning bush, we learn that God described himself in these terms: 'I am the God of Abraham and the God of Isaac and the God of Jacob.' At the time when these words are spoken Abraham, Isaac and Jacob are all long since dead. Now if death and Sheol are the last word, God ought to be saying something like this: 'When Abraham was alive I was his God; and so with Isaac and Jacob. I am ready to be to their descendants what I was to them in their day.' But that clearly will not do. The words actually used by God must mean that he cares for Abraham, Isaac and Jacob; and if he cares for them, they cannot be abandoned to the living death of the Sheol of Sadducean orthodoxy. Moreover if God cares for the patriarchs individually, we may make bold to believe that he cares for other people individually; and because he cares for them, they are safe in his hands. The God of Abraham, Isaac and Jacob

44

is also, and in the same full sense, the God of John Smith, William Brown and Henry Robinson. Because he cares for them one at a time they need no longer fear death. The basis of our Lord's teaching on life after death is the fact that God has a personal care for the individual human person.

So much for the teaching of Jesus. It is only a bare outline that can be offered here; but for our immediate purpose a statement of the essential points of the teaching may serve. We turn now to the resurrection of Jesus himself. Here again we can deal only in broad outlines. The big difference between the *Phaedo* and the Gospels is that while the *Phaedo* offers reasons for thinking that after death the soul of Socrates will continue to exist somewhere or somehow away from the entanglements of the material world, the Gospels give an account of the return of Jesus after death to rejoin his disciples, to stop their talking about him in the past tense, to revive the fellowship, and to continue his ministry in the world. The Church, which is his body, is the first corollary of his resurrection; and it is most right and proper that the last word of the Gospel should be, 'Lo, I am with you always, even to the end of the world.'

But that is not all. Along with this perpetual presence of Christ living on in the Church there goes the picture of the exalted Christ seated at the right hand of God in the heavenly places. The risen life of the Lord is life lived on two planes. This is something that we are not in a position to understand properly, much less to explain. It is something which we only begin to experience in the life of the Christian fellowship on this side of the grave. According to St Paul, the Christian in baptism dies with Christ and rises again into the life of Christ's body, the Church. So far he shares the resurrection-life of Christ in this world, on the mundane level. But, also according to St Paul, when the Christian dies he goes to be with Christ, that is, to share the resurrection-life of Christ on another level. For the Christian there is in this world a real, though necessarily limited, experience of the risen life of Christ.

The matter may perhaps be illustrated by an analogy. If we lived in a world of only two spatial dimensions, many things in the three-dimensional world would be simply incomprehensible to us. For example, if the picture of a man climbing a spiral staircase could be projected into our two-dimensional world he would seem to be walking round and round in a circle. If the projection was made from a different angle he would appear to be walking in a straight line. He would never appear to be doing what in fact he is doing, climbing up a staircase. The only way in which we could know the full truth of the matter would be by having the third dimension added to our experience.

I suspect it is something like this in the resurrection-life. It is not a case of losing a dimension – time for example: 'timeless life' is a contradiction in terms – but of gaining one; and to gain one is to open up vistas of experience as unimaginable to us now as climbing a spiral staircase would be to dwellers in two-dimensional space.

There is no end of speculations of this kind about the resurrection-life, and no harm in them. But all such speculations presuppose the resurrection faith; and, if I have understood the teaching of the Bible aright, that faith is always a corollary to the justice and love of our Father in heaven.

NOTES

1. 2 Sam. 12.19–23 (RSV).
2. *De rerum natura*, III, 838–42 (C. Bailey's translation).
3. E. F. Sutcliffe, *The Old Testament and the Future Life*, p. 6.
4. Sutcliffe, op. cit. p. 18.
5. *The Vitality of the Individual in the Thought of Ancient Israel*, p. 88ff.
6. J. Pedersen, *Israel I–II*, p. 460.
7. A. R. Johnson, op. cit. p. 93f.
8. This way of thinking persisted long. In the Talmud (Ned. 64b Bar) we are told of four classes of people who are considered as good as dead: the poor, the blind, the lepers and the childless. Again in *Sanh.*

T. W. Manson

47a Elisha's healing of Naaman's leprosy is equated with a raising from the dead. cf. Strack-Billerbeck, *Komm.* iv. 751.

9. F. M. Cornford, *Greek Religious Thought from Homer to the Age of Alexander*, xxiv. This devaluation of the sensible world and its life, with the escapist eschatology that flows from it, reappears in some early Christian thinking, especially in heretical – Gnostic and Marcionite – doctrine.

10. The issue has been stated clearly and uncompromisingly by L. P. Jacks in the opening chapter of his book, *Near the Brink*.

11. op. cit. pp. 131–7.

12. Matt. 27.52f. It is not necessary for our present purpose to discuss the question of the historicity of this particular detail.

13. Luke 16.19–31.

14. Mark 12.18–27, with parellels in Matt. 22.23–33; Luke 20.27–38.

15. I think I should mention here the comment which I heard given by my teacher, Herbert Loewe, on this phrase. He suggested that 'the power of God' is a reference to that very ancient part of the Synagogue liturgy, the Eighteen Benedictions, and in particular to the second of them, which is concerned with the resurrection. The text runs, 'Thou art mighty, who bringest low the proud; (thou art) strong and judgest the ruthless, living for ever thou raisest the dead, makest the wind to blow, sendest down the dew, sustainest the living, quickenest the dead; in the twinkling of an eye thou makest salvation to spring forth for us. Blessed art thou, O Lord, who quickenest the dead.' It is very significant that in this benediction which is so largely occupied with the activity of God in sustaining and restoring life to the world, he should be addressed in the very first clause as 'mighty'; and it is tempting to suppose that 'the power of God' in Mark is an echo of 'the mighty One' of the second Benediction. If this is so, the force of the remark is, 'You don't know either your Bible or your Prayer Book.'

I do not know whether Loewe ever published this very attractive suggestion: I cannot recall ever seeing it in print. I mention it here in order that it may not be forgotten and that he may have the credit for it.

16. This is perhaps the moment to mention that curiosity of patristic exegesis by which the Lucan form of the saying ἰσάγγελοι γάρ εἰσιν was interpreted to mean that the number of persons to be raised from death to life will be exactly equal to the number of angels who fell with Satan, and that in this way the host of heaven will be brought up to full strength. There is an echo of this interpretation in the Prayer Book service for the Burial of the Dead in the petition 'that it may please

thee . . . shortly to accomplish the number of thine elect'. cf. E. Evans, *Saint Augustine's Enchiridion*, 117.

17. Matt. 8.11f.; Luke 13.29.
18. Matt. 25.31–46.
19. I say this in spite of verse 46, which I am strongly inclined to regard as editorial comment. The proper climax has been reached in verse 45.

The Teaching of Jesus
Concerning the Future Life

H. T. ANDREWS

There can be little doubt that one of the great needs of the
Christian Church today is a reconstruction of its faith in the
future life. It is said that Hegel, though he was a firm believer
in the immortality of the soul, drew up his philosophical system without the slightest reference to this article of his creed.
Hegel is a symbol of most of us in modern times. We have
ceased to live *sub specie eternitatis*. And yet it is only a generation since George Eliot levelled against the Christian Church
the charge of otherworldliness and urged that it lived with
its head in the clouds, absorbed in the vision of the golden
streets of the New Jerusalem and altogether oblivious of the
needs of the present world. Modern Christianity took the
taunt of George Eliot very much to heart. It turned its gaze
from heaven to earth. Hell was blotted out of its vocabulary
and heaven became for many people a vague *terra incognita*
– almost as formless and void as the Hebrew Sheol. If Dante
were reincarnated in the modern world and baptized into
the spirit of the age the theme of his immortal poems might
very well have been a Utopia: it is inconceivable that he
would write a *Paradiso* or an *Inferno*. It seems quite certain
that we could not have written the great Christian hymns
of the future life if we had not inherited them from the past
and many of them sound strangely unreal when they proceed
from modern lips. We sing with Tennyson

> Thou wilt not leave us in the dust
> Thou madest man, he knows not why,

49

He thinks he was not made to die,
And Thou hast made him – Thou art just.

Though there is faith in words like these, it is faith set in
the minor key. It is not a faith that satisfies. It is a faith that
gropes its way in the dim twilight if haply it may lay hold
on eternal life – not a faith that marches with head erect
in the full sunlight of confident assurance to a triumphant
goal.

And it is because the eschatology of the Church lies today
between two worlds – 'one dead – one powerless to be born'
that multitudes of men and women are seeking from other
sources the help and guidance which it cannot, or at any
rate does not, give. It is the default of the Church that makes
recourse to psychical research so popular today. The thirst
for some sure token of the survival of the soul after death
is ineradicable in the human mind, and if the Church speaks
in halting or discordant tones people will inevitably go
elsewhere in their quest for some clear proof of immortality.
It has always been so. When the old pagan faiths of Greece
and Rome crumbled to pieces, when great Pan was dead,
the mystery religions arose, and men and women went to
them in shoals – because they held out the promise of the
hope of an after life. History has simply repeated itself in
these latter days.

The old eschatology of the Christian Church is dead. It
deserved to die. It could only live in the atmosphere of a
narrow and rigid Calvinism whose conception of God was
not unlike the portrait of Nebuchadnezzar in the book of
Daniel – 'Whom he would he slew and whom he would he
saved alive.' It cannot be resuscitated. The faith of today
could not tolerate it for a moment. But faith cannot live
without an eschatology; and it is one of the supreme tasks
of the hour to attempt to lay down the fundamental
principles of a new eschatology which shall be consonant
with all that is best in modern thought and yet shall have

all the confidence and assurance which characterized the faith of the past.

It will be generally admitted that a Christian eschatology must be based primarily upon the teaching of Jesus, and that it is to him we must turn for guidance and inspiration in our work of reconstruction. While it is possible to gain help and illumination from every honest investigation of the subject from Plato down to Sir Oliver Lodge, yet it is to Jesus we must always go as our ultimate authority in matters of faith and doctrine.

What then are the data which we can obtain from the teaching of Jesus as a basis for the task that lies before us? Now it is not as easy as a casual reader of the Gospels would suppose to obtain an answer to this question: there are many difficulties which we must overcome before we can feel that our feet are resting upon sure ground.

The first difficulty we have to face is the comparative reticence of Jesus on the subject of the future life. The Fourth Gospel makes Jesus apologize for this reticence. 'In my Father's house are many mansions. If it were not so I would have told you.' We look in vain in the Gospels for any description of heaven or of hell comparable to what we find in Homer or Plato or Virgil or Jewish Apocalyptic or the Apocalypse of Peter or Dante or in many forms of Christian art. This reticence is all the more remarkable when we remember that the whole world in the time of Jesus was obsessed as it had never been before in the whole course of its history by the problems of eschatology. No one can read the Jewish literature of the last two centuries BC without seeing how keen was the interest displayed in the doctrine of the future life and how many were the theories which were put forward by different writers as to its nature and character. The conceptions of heaven and hell which in later times dominated Christian thought were in all their essential features the creation of this Period. The rise and development of the Greek mysteries prove that the same interest was equally keen and vivid in the Græco-Roman world. The amazing thing is that in face of this vortex of discussion Jesus kept comparative silence and refused to be drawn into the debate.

The second difficulty that confronts us is the fact that throughout the Gospels Jesus speaks in terms of the Kingdom rather than in terms of the future life. The dominant idea in the teaching of Jesus is undoubtedly the establishment of the Kingdom of God on earth – the creation of an ideal human society in which the will of God shall be done on earth as perfectly as it is done in heaven. The thought of Jesus, especially as it is recorded in the Synoptists, revolves round the setting up of this Kingdom, and is mainly concerned with its nature and the character of its citizens, the conditions of entrance into it, and the grounds upon which men are excluded from its joys and glory. Now it may be asserted with every degree of confidence that the same principles which govern the establishment of an ideal society on the plane of earth govern also the entrance into the larger life of heaven. The very phrases that are used – 'The Kingdom of Heaven' – or 'The Kingdom of God' – show the essential community of ideas involved in the two conceptions. You cannot have two moral codes or two standards of righteousness, one for earth and the other for heaven. Whether the future life is to be spent in an earthly Utopia or in heaven, the tests by which a man is judged worthy of a place in either realm must inevitably be the same.

But it does not follow from this that the conditions in all their details must necessarily be identical. For instance, we are at any rate entitled to ask the question whether exclusion from the earthly Kingdom means absolute and final exclusion from a future life in heaven? Then, too, the doctrine of the resurrection as it appears in the New Testament (whatever may be its ultimate value for Christian faith) is much more relevant to the earthly Kingdom than it is to the future life. Directly the conception of a Kingdom of saints on earth entered into Hebrew belief the question was at once asked, What will be the fate of the good men who died before the Kingdom was established? Will they lose their chance of a share in the final triumph? And when the issue was raised faith could only give one reply to it. No: it is unthinkable to suppose that they will miss the prize: they will be raised to life again in order that they may have a place in the Kingdom. When the emphasis was shifted from an earthly Kingdom to a future life in heaven, the doctrine of the resurrection, as Paul found, had to be modified to suit the new conception. We must be careful, therefore, not to assume that everything which is said about the Kingdom on earth is necessarily applicable to the future life in heaven.

A further difficulty is connected with the fact that we cannot always be sure that we possess the actual words which Jesus used. It is remarkable[1] that at the crucial points of the discussion the language of the different Evangelists varies, and we are faced by the problem of having to choose between the different records. This applies particularly to the statements of Jesus about the punishment of the wicked. Matthew is the stronghold of the doctrine of eternal punishment. There are passages in Mark and Luke that imply this belief, but they are far fewer in number, and much less vivid and strong than they are in Matthew. There can be little doubt that Matthew has gone out of his way to intensify the teaching of Jesus upon this point. There are seven references to hell (Gehenna) in Matthew against one in Mark and one in Luke. The word 'eternal' is never used by Luke of future punishment and is found only once in Mark, while in Matthew the term is introduced on four occasions. When we compare the parable of the pounds in Luke and the parable of the talents in Matthew we find that the first ends on the note, 'Take the pound from him and give it to him that hath the ten pounds' – a perfectly natural ending – while Matthew adds the words, 'Cast ye out the unprofitable servant into the outer darkness, there shall be the weeping and gnashing of teeth' – a doom which seems altogether extravagant compared with the crime. We are compelled, therefore, to face the question, Has Luke softened down the teaching of Jesus or has Matthew intensified it? There can be little doubt that the second alternative is correct. And in the light of this evidence we are entitled to argue that the words in which Matthew summarizes the teaching of the parable of the great assize, 'These shall go away into eternal punishment, but the righteous into eternal life', are also an editorial addition. At any rate there is no escape from the variations in the evidence which constitute our third difficulty – and we have no right to assume that every saying attributed to Jesus by the evangelists is necessarily genuine.

But there is still a fourth difficulty which we must surmount if we are to succeed in our task. Much of the terminology which Jesus uses in his references to the future life according to the report of his sayings in the Evangelists is simply the conventional language of his time. During the intermediate period between the Old and New Testaments – which was really the creative period for the development of eschatology – a new set of terms had come into existence and passed into common speech. Most of them are mere metaphors. Gehenna, for instance, is simply the valley of Hinnom – where the dead bodies of criminals and the refuse of Jerusalem were burned – transferred to another plane. The 'outer darkness' is merely a phrase which symbolizes exclusion from the joy and brightness of the banqueting-hall. In evolving the phraseology of the future life the Jewish Apocalyptic writers were bound to interpret the unknown in terms of the known and to make use of the best illustration available in the language of the time. Much of the language which Jesus is said to have used on the question of the after life – most of it in fact – is not of his own making. He simply uses the current coinage of his age. As far as the terms are concerned there is scarcely a new word or even a new idea used by Jesus in his actual eschatological utterances. He employs the metaphors which were in common use at the time. The crime which the old eschatology committed consisted in regarding the conventional language which Jesus was compelled to use as his own great contribution to the subject, and partly in turning poetry into prose and hardening metaphor into dogma. The vale of Hinnom may have been a very good metaphor for describing the place where the wicked are to be punished, but it is only a metaphor after all and it must be treated as a metaphor. To take it literally, and to regard it as a microcosm of the scene of future punishment – and that is how it had come to be taken in the days of Christ – is to provide another illustration of the truth of the great saying of St Paul, 'The letter killeth but the spirit giveth life.' It is not, it cannot be too emphatically urged, what Jesus has in common with the eschatological language and thought of his time that constitutes the substance of his revelation on the future life. It is rather in the words he utters on rare occasions which do not reflect the vocabulary of his age and which even come into conflict with much of the current conventional eschatology that the truth of his own great message is to be found.

A critical examination of the data at our disposal in the Gospels leads us to the following conclusions.

A strong and invincible belief in the future life is the postulate of the whole of the teaching of Jesus. To him the conviction of immortality is axiomatic. There is no doubt or hesitation about it at all. He never – except on one solitary occasion – argues about it. Addison can say of the argument of the *Phaedo:*

> It must be so – Plato, thou reasonest well.
> Else whence this pleasing hope, this fond desire,
> This longing after immortality?

But we cannot use words like these about the teaching of Jesus on the future life. He speaks with authority. Plato talks like a scribe. Jesus speaks about the life to come as he speaks about God. You may search the Gospels in vain for any trace of the theistic proofs. Jesus knows nothing of the great arguments – the cosmological, the teleological, the ontological – by which later apologists sought to demonstrate the existence of God. He speaks out of his own instinctive knowledge, both about the nature of God and the nature of the future life. The only occasion when he ventures upon an argument about the life to come is in reply to the question of the Sadducees about the resurrection (Mark 12.26f): 'As touching the dead, that they are raised; have ye not read in the book of Moses, in the place concerning the Bush, how God spake unto him saying, "I am the God of Abraham and the God of Isaac and the God of Jacob." He is not the God of the dead but of the living.' An appeal to the Pentateuch does not seem to us today to be very convincing, whatever it may have been in the first century. And yet as Canon Streeter has said:[2] 'It is much more than an *argumentum ad hominem*. To say that God is the God of Abraham and Isaac and Jacob is to say that he is a God who sets a supreme value on individual persons and it is argued that the fact that God so values them is a guarantee that he cannot allow them to perish. It is essentially an argument from the character of God: and its point and cogency lies in the assertion that belief in immortality is a necessary deduction and consequence of a right belief in God.'

Whether Canon Streeter's exegesis of this particular passage is sound or not may be a matter of opinion, but there can be no question at all that a belief in immortality is necessarily implied in the teaching of Jesus about God and man. How could Jesus have believed in the infinite love of God for the sons of men without also believing in an eternal destiny for the human soul? How could he have believed in the infinite worth of each individual life? How could he have said that it is not the will of God that one of these little ones should perish – unless he had also believed that death was not the final end of things and that man is not like the beasts that perish? The words that Jesus spoke about immortality may be few, but the doctrine is woven into the whole fabric of his thought and teaching, and without it the rest of his theology would be robbed of more than half its value. It is the postulate – the fundamental assumption – upon which all that he said about God and man depends. It was no meaningless phrase when a later writer asserted that Jesus 'abolished death and brought life and immortality to light'.

Apart from the revelation of Christ the belief in immortality could not by the very nature of the case be more than a sublime hypothesis – an act of faith that leaps over the barriers that limit the progress of human reason. The feeling of the inadequacy of human reasoning to attain to certainty is present even in the *Phaedo* of Plato:[3] at a point in the discussion when a particular line of proof is shown to have failed in its demonstration, one of the interlocutors says: 'Well then, all that we can do is to take the best and most unanswerable arguments that we can find and use them as a kind of raft to carry us through the perils of the sea of life, till some word of god affords us a surer basis for our faith.' That cry – Messianic in its intensity – for some authoritative word of God to set all doubts at rest was answered by Jesus, who in his teaching and in his resurrection gave the world a sure token of the life to come and transformed for Christians at any rate the sublime hypothesis into a glorious certainty.

But what has Jesus to tell us about the content of the Christian hope? What does the life to come mean upon his lips? The classic description of the heavenly life is given in John 14, the passage which has brought greater comfort to timid and sorrowful souls throughout the centuries than any other passage in the Bible. 'In my Father's house are many mansions... I go to prepare a place for you that where I am ye may be also. And if I go and prepare a place for you I will come again and receive you to myself.' If it be objected that at this time of the day, in the light of the critical discussion of the sources, it is unscientific to quote as authentic a saying of Jesus which is only found in the Fourth Gospel, my answer is that of Matthew Arnold. The sayings of Jesus in the supper table discourses 'cannot in the main be the writer's, because in the main they are quite beyond his reach'. It seems to me that Matthew Arnold's argument is unassailable. We have in 1 John ample material for a psychological study of the mind of the writer of the Fourth Gospel. We know all about his mental outlook and his theological position. His method and manner of thought are an open book to us. We know that there are many things attributed to Jesus in the discourses of the Fourth Gospel which he could have written – and probably did write – out of his own inner consciousness. But we also know that there are other things which by no stretch of imagination can be supposed to be the creation of his own intellect – and among these not the least important is the opening paragraph of the fourteenth chapter. There is no indication at all in the Epistle that he could himself have risen to the heights of the great words he ascribes to Jesus. His conception of the future life is set in a different key. He can write the words, 'Beloved now are we the children of God and it doth not yet appear what we shall be. We know that if he be manifested we shall be like him for we shall see him face to face': but it would have been quite beyond his capacity to have invented the great utterance, 'In my Father's house are many mansions. I go to prepare a place for you.'

The first thing that strikes us about these words of Jesus is their remarkable simplicity. There is no trace of the complex idea of the seven heavens so familiar to Jewish thought. There is no hint of the gorgeous vision of the eternal city which filled the mind of the author of Revelation, with its golden streets and its jasper walls and its gates of precious stone. There is nothing to suggest the description of heaven which is given in the Apocalypse of Peter – 'a great space shining with brilliant light and blooming with unfading flowers and full of spices and sweet smelling plants, incorruptible and

bearing a blessed fruit, and a perfume that spread far beyond
the boundaries of the land.' Jesus paints no elaborate picture
of heaven – but by a single stroke of the pen he gives us a
much more satisfying conception of it than we can find in
the luscious visions of the apocalyptists and the imaginative
art of medieval painters. Heaven to Jesus is the Father's
house. 'The Father's house'! There is a divine simplicity
about the phrase – and yet it is infinitely more eloquent than
the luxuriant word-painting in which lesser minds have
always indulged when they came to speak of heaven. The
future life is, as the Apostle Paul once put it, 'to be at home
with God'. And lest it be felt that translation to so sublime
a sphere, even though it be the Father's house, may be
strange and startling to the soul, Jesus adds the words, 'I go
to prepare a place for you.' The new environment is adjusted
to the needs of the individual soul. Each will be assigned the
position in which he will feel most at home with God.

And this brings me to the next point. In the conception
of Jesus there is an absolute continuity between this life and
the next. Whatever transformation may take place in our
passage to the eternal world it will not destroy the identity
of our personality. What will live after us is not some shadowy
ghost or some weird spectral phantom. What will enter into
the life of the other world will be the personality which we
have made for ourselves in the life that now is. The Fourth
Gospel is quite right when it regards eternal life as a present
fact. 'He that believeth on me hath everlasting life . . . He that
hath the son hath life . . . This is eternal life, that they may
know thee the only true God, and him whom thou didst send
even Jesus Christ.' The Fourth Gospel is only making explicit
what is implicit in the teaching of the Synoptics. Even
Aristotle feels that immortality must begin here and now.
In a famous passage in the *Nicomachean Ethics*[4] he writes:
'If then reason be divine compared with human nature,
so too the life which consists in the exercise of reason
will also be divine in comparison with ordinary human life.

Therefore instead of listening to those who urge us as men and mortals not to lift our thoughts above what is human and mortal, we ought as far as is possible to us to live as the immortals and act in accordance with the highest principle we possess.' Aristotle's advice that we should 'practise immortality' or live the immortal life on earth is entirely consonant with the teaching of Jesus. There can be no dualism between the life on earth and the life in heaven. The life in heaven will be the fruition and the reward of life on the plane of earth. The main point of difference between Jesus and Aristotle would, I think, be this. To Aristotle it is only the rational principle, the thinking part, of the man that survives death; to Jesus it is the whole personality. The immortal soul to Aristotle is that element in man that thinks and reasons; to Jesus it is the whole of the higher self, the self that feels and wills and loves as well as reasons. Eternal life to Aristotle is the sublimation of mind and thought: to Jesus it is the sublimation of all that is best and noblest in human life. Heaven to Aristotle is a kind of celestial university in which those who have acquitted themselves well in the schools of earth will take a post-graduate course of eternal duration; to Jesus it is a home which provides opportunity for the development of those moral capacities which constitute the highest part of human personality.

It follows from what has been said that there are different planes of life in heaven as there are on earth. If we are to begin the next life very much at the point at which we leave this life – and that is a necessary assumption if we are to maintain the identity of personality – it is quite clear that we are weaving at the looms of time the garment which we shall wear when we enter on the life of heaven. Time after time in his teaching Jesus emphasizes the fact that the present life determines our destiny. He urges men to 'lay up for themselves treasure in heaven'. He says of certain types of conduct and of men that 'great will be their reward in heaven'. He condemns the imprudence and lack of foresight in the sons

of light as compared with the farseeing policy of the Unjust
Steward and bids them 'Make for yourselves friends from
the mammon of unrighteousness that when it fails they may
receive you into the eternal habitations.' He denounces those
who live without a thought of the eternal world. And yet
with all his talk about rewards Jesus is careful to teach us
that heaven is the gift of God's grace and cannot be earned
by the works of men. That is the meaning of the parable of
the Labourers in the Vineyard, who all, irrespective of the
length of their service, receive at the end of the day the same
reward. This parable does not cancel all that Jesus says in
other places about 'the treasure in heaven'. It is only intended to show that human merit is not the main factor that
secures the heavenly reward.

> Merit lives from man to man
> And not from man, O God, to Thee.

'Salvation,' as Dr Fairbairn used to put it, 'is always of
grace and reward is of works.' There must inevitably be at
the heavenly judgement a great reversal of human verdicts.
'The last will be first and the first will be last.' The record
of the history of the Church as it is written in the books of
heaven will read very differently from the narrative to which
we are accustomed. Some of the great names which are
blazoned on the pages of our story may occupy a very lowly
place in the final narrative, and many a nameless un-
remembered saint will receive the meed of praise that the
purblind historians of earth have denied to him.

It has been said that it is not what the teaching of Jesus
contains in common with conventional eschatology of his age
that constitutes his real contribution to the doctrine of the
future life – it is rather when he breaks loose from the current
ideas and phraseology of his times that he illuminates most
clearly the character of the heavenly life. Another of these
few original utterances is found in the words in the parable
of the Talents addressed by the master to the servants who

have proved worthy of their trust: 'Well done, good and
faithful servant: thou hast been faithful over a few things;
I will set thee over many things; enter thou into the joy of
thy Lord.' It is not so much the words of congratulation and
the promotion to tasks of higher responsibility that constitute
the real significance of the words: it is rather the final clause
– 'Enter thou into the joy of thy Lord.' The word used is
joy not *happiness*. That there will be happiness in the life of
heaven goes without saying. But *joy* is a different and a
greater thing. The distinction in the meaning of the two
words has been well brought out by the French philosopher,
Bergson. 'Happiness,' he says, 'is the response of the soul to
a congenial environment ... Joy is the symbol of creation
... Where joy is creation must have been ... Nature has set
up a sign which apprizes us every time our activity is in full
expansion. This sign is joy. True joy is always an emphatic
signal of the triumph of life. Wherever joy is creation has
been and the richer the creation the greater the joy.' If Bergson is right heaven will be the sphere not merely of activity
but of creative work. And it will be creative work of the
highest order – 'the joy of the Lord'. The joy of Jesus was
supreme because he had achieved the greatest of all creative
works – the redemption of mankind. And into the joy of that
high purpose the Christian will enter in the heavenly life.
And all the faltering efforts of our present life, 'the high that
proved too high – the heroic for earth too hard' will be translated into the perfect realization of heaven.

It is not easy for us, engrossed and absorbed as we are in
the pursuits which are imposed upon us by the conditions
of life on the plane of earth, to form any conception of the
work that lies before us in the other world. We are compelled
to toil now in the interest of physical life and well being.
Much of our strength is spent in labouring for the meat that
perisheth. It almost passes our comprehension to imagine a
world where we shall be emancipated from the struggle for
physical existence and set free for the higher tasks of the spiri-

tual life. For Jesus has left us in no doubt that the life of the world to come will be entirely spiritual. In answer to the problem which the Sadducees put to him as a *reductio ad absurdum* of all belief in a future life, Jesus said with the utmost emphasis, 'Ye do err, not knowing the scripture, nor the power of God. For in the resurrection they neither marry nor are given in marriage, but are as the angels in heaven.' It is notable that in this passage Jesus uses the idea of resurrection. Apart from the parallel passages in the other Synoptic Gospels the only other reference to the resurrection in the Synoptic record occurs in Luke 14.14, 'Thou shalt be recompensed in the resurrection of the just.' These allusions are not sufficient to prove that Jesus held the view of the resurrection depicted in Revelation: 'And the sea gave up the dead which were in it and death and Hades gave up the dead that were in them and they were judged every man according to their works.' There is, of course, the strange passage in John 5: 'The hour cometh in which all that are in the tombs shall hear his voice and shall come forth, they that have done good unto the resurrection of life and they that have done ill unto the resurrection of judgement.' But that passage is so diametrically opposed to the spirit and teaching of the Fourth Gospel and finds so little to support it in the other records of the teaching of Jesus – that an increasing number of modern scholars regard it as an interpolation and deny that it represents the position of Jesus at all. The whole tenor of the teaching of Jesus is dead against the theory that death is followed by a long sleep in an attenuated life in Hades, until the last trumpet sounds. Lazarus in the parable goes at once to Abraham's bosom, and Dives is taken immediately to his doom in Hades. Jesus says to the dying thief upon the cross, 'This day shalt thou be with me in Paradise.' St Paul in earlier days when he was writing 1 Thessalonians seems to have held the belief that death was followed by a sleep till the second coming of Christ, but he soon found such an idea to be intolerable, and he had the courage to abandon his first view and declare that 'to be absent from the body is to be present with the Lord'. There is no real justification in the teaching of Jesus for the picture of the resurrection drawn in Revelation, and it is a great pity that that book should ever have been allowed to cast its fell shadow over the Christian hope, for in this matter as in some others it represents the triumph of Jewish Apocalyptic over the Christian faith and not the triumph of the Christian faith over Jewish Apocalyptic. It cannot be said too emphatically that it is impossible to extract a uniform eschatology out of the pages of the New Testament, and when it comes to a clash between the teaching of Jesus and the teaching of Revelation, the Christian theologian has no choice open to him but to accept the authority of the Master rather than that of one of his later disciples – a disciple who learnt far more from Jewish Apocalyptic than he did from Christ himself. The time has come when it ought to be said quite frankly that there are some elements in the New Testament – in 1 Thessalonians and in Revelation for instance – which are quite out of harmony with the spirit of the teaching of Jesus, and which ought not to be regarded as a true expression of the Christian hope.

But what of the other side of the problem? What of the fate of the wicked? There is nothing in the New Testament to justify the facile optimism of the modern world. On the other hand there is a sternness, a moral severity, about the teaching of Jesus which is often overlooked, and which we have allowed to be submerged in the sense of the love and gentleness and pity of the Christ. 'How different,' says Thomas Carlyle, 'is the honeymouthed tear-stained Jesus of the modern Christian from the stern-visaged Christ of the Gospels proclaiming aloud in the market-place, "Woe unto you scribes and Pharisees, hypocrites!"' Jesus is wonderfully pitiful. 'The bruised reed he will not break, the smoking flax he will not quench'; but he is also terribly stern. 'Whosoever shall cause one of these little ones that believe on me to stumble, it were better for him that a great millstone were hanged about his neck and he were cast into the sea. And if thy hand cause thee to stumble cut it off and cast it from thee; it is good for thee to enter into life maimed rather than having two hands to go into hell – into the unquenchable fire.'

Into the details of the discussion about the meaning of these terrible sayings it is impossible for us to enter now. All that can be said is that when we have eliminated from the Gospels the passages which individual Evangelists – especially Matthew – may have added on their own authority to the record of the teaching of Jesus; when we have taken the word αἰώνιος (which is generally translated eternal) and proved from its derivation and its usage in the literature of the time that it does not necessarily mean 'everlasting'; when we have weighed the possibility that some of these sayings may refer only to the earthly Kingdom and not to the future life; when we have tried to lay bare the meaning of the metaphorical terms that Jesus uses and have translated them from the realm of the physical to the realm of the spiritual – there are still two statements that cannot lightly be explained away. There is first of all the statement about the unforgivable sin, the sin which cannot be pardoned in this world or the next. This cannot be an interpolation by an individual Evangelist, since it is one of the best authenticated sayings of Jesus in the Gospels, being found in the original source of Matthew and Luke which is generally known as Q and also in Mark. There is one crumb of comfort that can be obtained from the passage. If there is one sin that cannot be pardoned in this world or the next we are entitled to draw the inference that there are other sins which may be pardoned in the after life. But the main statement itself is very difficult to explain away. And yet if there ever was a sin against the Holy Spirit it was the sin of the men who caused Jesus to be crucified. It is difficult to imagine a more heinous form of this sin than the tragic miscarriage of justice which led to the death upon the Cross. And yet Jesus prays for the men who compassed his death, 'Father, forgive them, for they know not what they do.' If that sin could be forgiven – and Jesus obviously thought it could – it is difficult to conceive of any sin which is beyond the scope of the grace of God.

The other passage is in the parable of Dives and Lazarus. When Dives in the anguish of Hades prays, 'Father Abraham, have mercy on me and send Lazarus that he may dip the tip of his finger in water and cool my tongue, for I am in anguish in this flame,' Abraham replies, 'Son, remember that in thy lifetime thou receivedst the good things and Lazarus the evil things – and beside all this, between us and you there is a great gulf fixed that they which would pass from us to you may not be able, and that none may cross over from you to us.' The statement about the impassable gulf that divides heaven from hell seems quite definite and absolute, and we cannot cavalierly put it on one side on the ground that the details of the story of the parable must never be pressed, because it seems to be an essential fact in the illustration. And yet if we are to believe the statement of 1 Peter which became an article in the creed of the Catholic Church, that impassable gulf was bridged by Christ himself, who after his death went and preached to 'the spirits in prison'. If the faith of the Church is right – if that gulf was bridged by Christ – it is no longer impassable. If in the light of some of the recorded sayings of Jesus we ask with one of the disciples, 'Who then can be saved?', the answer comes, 'With men it is impossible but not with God, for all things are possible with God.' It is on that phrase – 'All things are possible with God' – that our faith in the final victory of God must ultimately rest, especially when we link it up with Luke's description of the good shepherd who goes after the lost sheep *until* he finds it. But it must be repeated there is no ground at all in the teaching of Jesus for the complacent and facile optimism so prevalent today – that optimism which so lightheartedly asserts that God is very good and very merciful and no matter what the character of our life on earth may be, all will come right at the last. At long last, yes, we trust it may – for we pin our faith to the belief that in the final issue not one life 'will be cast as rubbish to the heap'. But long last is an eternity away. To suppose that love makes God morally indifferent to what we have been and what we have done on earth is a travesty of the New Testament faith. It has been said of our present life that 'when youth is a blunder, manhood is a struggle and old age is a regret'. A misspent youth handicaps a man's whole career and makes success, if not impossible, at any rate desperately difficult. And the misspent life on earth must inevitably mean tragedy in the life to come – a tragedy of sorrow and anguish of soul – and desperate efforts after repentance and purity of heart without which no one can ever behold the vision of God. No: the moral we must draw from the teaching of Jesus is not the moral of optimistic complacency; it is rather the moral that Paul drew, 'I have suffered the loss of all things and count them but refuse that I may gain Christ and be found in Him . . . if by any means I may attain unto the resurrection of the dead.'

NOTES

1. More remarkable I think in the case of eschatology than in the case of any other theme upon which Jesus spoke.
2. B. H. Streeter, *Immortality*, p. 79.
3. 85 CD.
4. x. 7§8.

Immortality and Resurrection

C. K. BARRETT

The subject I am obliged to handle in this lecture, which, in terms of its foundation, must deal with the soul's destiny, and the nature and reality of the life hereafter, is one that must needs evoke a good deal of anxiety in a lecturer who has a strong preference for subjects about which he is not entirely ignorant. Is there a subject that grips human imagination so tenaciously, and exercises the human spirit so deeply, as this one? And is there a subject where, I do not say the heathen, but the Christian, nourished in the revealed truths of his religion, is so completely uninformed? *That* Christ was raised from the dead, and raised as the first-fruits of those who have fallen asleep, he may well believe; but, even at the cost of incurring Paul's rebuke, he may still find himself asking: 'But how are the dead raised, and with what kind of body do they come?'

There are questions to which we do not know the answers which it may, nevertheless, be profitable and edifying to discuss, and I do not propose simply to run away from the direct inquiry: 'If a man die, shall he live again?' I do, however, beg leave to approach it in my own way, and my way is not that of a philosopher or dogmatic theologian, but that of a historian. I shall have my feet firmly and reassuringly planted in this world if I may at least begin by inquiring and recounting what men have felt, believed, and said (and what they have said is to be found not only in works of theology, but in plays and pictures, on tombstones and in burial vaults) about what happens to them when they die. It may be that, at least for some, this will prove not only to be of historical value but also to provide as good a starting-point for our own thinking, and as practical a setting for our own faith, as a more philosophical discourse might afford.

Our historical study has all the more chance of issuing in a positive and useful result because it will have the New Testament at its centre. It would be easy indeed to fill the whole of a lecture with New Testament exegesis: there is plenty of material, and the material affords problems enough to keep the exegete busy, and substance enough to provide for the systematic theologian – to say nothing of the support it offers to the trembling mortal (whether theologian or not) who stands on the river's brink. But I intend (even though this means abjuring detail) to investigate a wider field: to look into some of the antecedents of the New Testament, and to ask what the next generations made of the New Testament.

I can best introduce my sketch in this way. For a generation or so it has been popular to draw a sharp contrast between the idea of immortality, and that of resurrection. The immortality of the soul, we have been told, is a philosopher's toy, with no better foundation than human speculation; not merely insubstantial, therefore, but positively misleading, since it encourages man to find his eternal security in himself and not in God. The resurrection of the body, however, can be only the act of God; it is the divine miracle, exemplified in the resurrection of Christ himself, in which alone the Christian can properly put his trust. Christians, it is said, do not believe in the immortality of the soul, but in resurrection at the last day. This sharp distinction is often coupled with the distinction between Greek and Hebrew: the Greeks believed in immortality, which is wrong; the Hebrews believed in resurrection, which is right.

An outstanding exponent of these views is Oscar Cullmann. In referring to him I must first of all say that in his lecture *Immortality of the Soul or Resurrection of the Dead?* (London, 1958) there is very much that any serious student of the New Testament must accept. Indeed, I suspect that Dr

Cullmann takes a little too warmly, and attaches too much importance to, some of the criticisms of the original (Swiss) publication of his work. A great deal of it strikes the reader as familiar, and in many respects I am in agreement with him. I have, however, ventured to express a point of significant difference by using in my title not his disjunctive 'or' but the conjunctive 'and' – Immortality and Resurrection. But in saying so much I am anticipating my conclusion, and for this we are not yet ready.

For the erroneous notion of the immortality of the soul Dr Cullmann blames the Greeks. That we can respect and admire both Plato and Paul 'is no reason for denying a radical difference between the Christian expectation of the resurrection of the dead and the Greek belief in the immortality of the soul'.[1] Repeatedly Dr Cullmann refers to the 'Greek concept of the immortality of the soul'. In this expression there is concealed a serious over-simplification of the facts.

Early Greeks and early Hebrews were markedly similar in their outlook upon physical death and what lay beyond it. This is in fact well-known ground, and I need not linger over it. For both, death was the end of worth-while existence. For the Hebrew, this meant Sheol, an undesirable abode of wretched shades.

> The dead know not anything, neither have they any more a reward; for the memory of them is forgotten. As well their love, as their hatred and their envy, is now perished; neither have they any more a portion for ever in anything that is done under the sun . . . there is no work, nor device, nor knowledge, nor wisdom, in Sheol, whither thou goest (Eccles. 9.5, 6, 10).

> As the cloud is consumed and vanisheth away,
> So he that goeth down to Sheol shall come up no more.
> He shall return no more to his house,
> Neither shall his place know him any more. (Job 7.9–10)

The Greeks thought of the underworld, the home of departed spirits, in a very similar way. Life and memory did indeed persist. This is part of the tragedy of the situation. In one of the most famous scenes in the *Odyssey* (xi. 465–540), Odysseus, permitted to visit the shades, addresses the dead Achilles, 'than whom no man, before or after, was more fortunate'.

> Formerly, in your lifetime, we Argives used to honour you equally with the gods, and now that you are here you exercise great power over the dead. Do not grieve about it, Achilles, now that you are dead.
>
> He answered, Do not make light of death to me, noble Odysseus. I would rather be on earth a serf to a landless man, with small enough living for himself, than act as king over all these dead men who have perished. (484–91)

So far the thought of the primitive Hebrew runs parallel with that of the primitive Greek. We can take a further step. Each was capable of imagining a 'standing up of corpses' (as Hoskyns used to say ἀνάστασις νεκρῶν should be rendered, if we wish to feel the original force of the words), but each imagined it only to reject it. Such things did not, and presumably could not, happen. We have already seen some of the Old Testament evidence. More can be added.

> Wilt thou shew wonders to the dead?
> Shall the shades arise(LXX, ἀναστήσουσιν and praise thee?
> Shall thy loving kindness be declared in the grave?
> Or thy faithfulness in Abaddon?
> Shall thy wonders be known in the dark?
> And thy righteousness in the land of forgetfulness?

There is also David's explanation of his composure when he learns of the death of Bathsheba's child.

While the child was yet alive, I fasted and wept; for I said, Who knoweth whether the Lord will not be gracious to me, that the child may live? But now he is dead, wherefore should I fast? Can I bring him back again? I shall go to him, but he shall not return to me (2 Sam. 12. 22–3).

In a similar way the Greeks speak of the rising up of the dead as something that no one supposes can or will ever happen, even though the mind can conceive it (as it can conceive other absurdities). Thus Prexaspes to Cambyses:

I did what you commanded me, and buried him with my own hands. If dead men do rise up (*εἰ μέν νυν οἱ τεθνεῶτες ἀνεστέασι*) you can expect Astyages the Mede to rise up against you; but if things continue as they have been you will never have any further trouble from him [Smerdis] (Herodotus, 3.62).

Other writers reveal the same scepticism. Thus Achilles to Priam, when the latter comes to beg for the body of his dead son, Hector.

You will achieve nothing by lamenting for your son, nor will you raise him up (*οὐδέ μιν ἀνστήσεις*) (*Iliad*, xxiv. 550f).

With this we may compare David's despair of his dead child. Again, when the Chorus suspects the death of Agamemnon

I have no means of raising up the dead again in words (Aeschylus, *Agamemnon* 1360f).

And similarly Sophocles: Electra will never succeed in raising her dead father from Hades.

But never by laments or prayers will you raise up (*ἀνστάσεις* your father from the lake of Hades to which all go (*Electra* 137ff).

Thus, if we go back to the earliest stages of their histories and literatures, we find Greeks and Hebrews thinking alike about death, and what happens after it. A living dog is better than a dead lion; a living serf is better than a dead king – they are agreed in this. Survival of a sort there is, but it is so wretched and poor that it would almost be better that existence should cease altogether.

It is true that neither Hebrews nor Greeks remained in this primitive stage and that subsequent developments did not follow identical lines. It is a commonplace observation that only towards the close of the Old Testament period was the national hope of a future for the people partially re-placed, or supplemented, by the personal hope of a future for the individual Israelite. There are only a few passages in the Old Testament where this hope appears unmistakably.

Many of them that sleep in the dust of the earth shall awake, some to everlasting life, and some to shame and everlasting contempt (Daniel 15.2).

Thy dead shall live; my dead bodies shall arise. Awake and sing, ye that dwell in the dust: for thy dew is as the dew of light, and the earth shall cast forth the shades (Isaiah 26.9).

After the close of the Old Testament period evidence multi-plies, and for the moment one passage will suffice as illustra-tion:

They that fear the Lord shall rise to life eternal,
And their life shall be in the light of the Lord, and shall
come to an end no more (Ps. Sol. 3.16).

It is often said that this new belief in resurrection to a new life in a new age came into Judaism from without, and especi-ally from Persian sources, whence the idea was borrowed. I should certainly not wish to deny that Iranian influence can be detected in the later parts of the Old Testament and in post-biblical Judaism; but I believe that Dr Mowinckel is right in saying that 'Persian influence served as a catalyst'.[2] The real constituents of the late Jewish belief lay within the earlier religion, and fundamentally in the conviction that he who was the judge of the whole earth would not fail to do right.[3] We can see in the earlier wisdom literature how a growing individualism raised problems for those who held to this conviction, and these problems were brought to a head when Jewish martyrs accepted death, thereby renouncing all hope of earthly reward and any direct share in the national hope, precisely in order to maintain the national religion. It was in this context that Daniel 12.2 (and possibly Isaiah 26.19) arose, and must be understood. In other words, it was in the light of human experience, illuminated by fundamental convictions about God, that Hebrew thought about man's future developed: Persian belief provided the mould into which this developing thought was poured rather than an essential constituent of the thought itself. In this process we cannot name any one outstanding thinker of unique personal insight and influence; not even the author of Daniel would qualify for such a description.

Not least at this point the Greek line of development differs markedly from the Hebrew; here there arises a figure so outstanding that even Dr Cullmann can speak of 'the Greeks' and 'Plato' almost as if these were interchangeable terms. This they certainly were not, for dominating as the Socrates-Plato figure is to us, it was probably unknown to and without direct influence upon the majority of 'Greeks' in the Hellenistic world. As with Jewish developments, so here we must probably bear in mind the presence of non-indigenous (that is, non-Hellenic) religious beliefs, particularly the influence of Orphism. But I venture to think that, as in Judaism, the really decisive force is to be found elsewhere. It is surely no accident that the essential development of Plato's thought about personal future life is to be found in the dialogues that deal with the martyr-figure of Socrates. Plato's thought follows a more intellectual and less purely religious course than that which led to the development we have noted in Judaism. He does not argue: Socrates was unjustly condemned, and since he refused to take the opportunity that presented itself to escape the hemlock in this world we must suppose that he will receive true justice hereafter. Rather Socrates appears as the human instrument of those ideas whose eternity points to the immortality of the human soul: 'There is no change in him; only now he is invested with a sort of sacred character, as the prophet or priest of Apollo the God of the festival, in whose honour he first of all composes a hymn, and then like the swan pours forth his dying lay. Perhaps the extreme elevation of Socrates above his own situation, and the ordinary interests of life (compare his *jeu d'esprit* about his burial, in which for a moment he puts on the "Silenus mask") create in the mind of the reader an impression stronger than could be derived from arguments that such an one, in his own language, has in him "a principle which does not admit of death".'[4]

We must not, as I have said, make the mistake of supposing that every Greek was a Plato, believing in the eternity of ideas and the immortality of the soul. Many in the ancient world had, as the inscriptions show, no hope for the future.

Non fui, fui, non sum, non curo.
πεῖνε, βλέπις τὸ τέλος

The badly spelt Greek points out the common man, and attests his belief – or unbelief. So far as hope penetrated to the unintellectual levels it did so by way of the cults; and it is well to remember that these rested in great measure upon a cycle, natural, mythological, or both, of death and resurrection.

Conditions in Palestine may not have been altogether different, but the Jews were an instructed people, and the more advanced beliefs of Pharisaic intellectuals probably spread farther downwards into society than Platonic speculation spread in the Greek world. And of the Pharisees Dr

Schweizer has rightly written: 'The Pharisees believed in the immortality of the soul *and* in the resurrection. Both conceptions are so formulated that they are not mutually exclusive.'[5] That they believed in resurrection appears from the passage in the Psalms of Solomon that I have already quoted. And according to Josephus the Pharisees hold that 'every soul is imperishable, but the soul of the good alone passes into another body, while the souls of the wicked suffer eternal punishment'.[6] We need not dismiss this as simply Josephus's hellenistic version of the Hebrew doctrine of the resurrection of the body. Instead of cumbering this lecture with references I will simply quote Billerbeck: 'Of no less significance for the earlier conceptions of Sheol [than the separation of righteous and wicked in Sheol] was the doctrine of immortality, which, from hellenistic Judaism, gradually pressed into Palestinian circles too.'[7] The same observation would probably be true with reference also to the Qumran type of Judaism.[8]

To sum up so far: we are guilty of an over-simplification so radical as to amount to falsification if we suggest that the background of New Testament thought about the future life is composed of 'Greeks' maintaining in intellectual terms the intrinsic immortality of the individual soul, and 'Hebrews' believing that at death man's whole being is extinguished and that he is miraculously raised up, body and soul, by God at the last day. The facts are far more complicated, and the distinction far less clear-cut. For both Greeks and Hebrews the common substratum of belief was the conception of Hades or Sheol – continuing, but quite undesirable existence. Many Greeks, and at least some Hebrews (the Sadducees as a matter of principle) did not go beyond this. Greek intellectuals developed the notion of immortality; Jewish mystics and apocalyptists looked for the resurrection of dead bodies. But many Jews believed at the same time in the immortality of what we may call the soul (whether they called it the soul or something else scarcely matters); and,

on the other side, we must remember that Greeks could at
any rate conceive the idea of rising up, that the cults were
based on a death-resurrection cycle, that the Stoic belief in
an ἐκπύρωσις and renewal of the universe involved something like resurrection, and that a similar implication may
be found in the Orphic and Pythagorean notion of the transmigration and reincarnation of souls.

That the New Testament emerged from this background
with a new and powerful conviction of life beyond the grave
was due neither to some chance turn of the wheel in the
syncretistic mixing-machine, nor to a new theory of the
nature of the soul, the nature of the body, or the relation
of the one to the other, but to the life, death, and resurrection of Jesus Christ. Jesus was dead, and is alive for ever-
more: this is the unanimous conviction of the New Testament
and the fact has consequences far wider than the subject at
present under discussion, important as that is. It means that
God has acted in history to deal with the total human situation, in which death is a symptom, with sin as its more fundamental cause. The death and resurrection of Jesus are repre-
sented by the New Testament writers as the means of God's
decisive victory over the powers of evil, but they are never,
I believe, used to vindicate one theory of body and soul
against another; they issue in the defeat of death, but this
fact does not in itself provide a history of what happens to
a man after the death of his body. Here as in other fields
men were left to bear witness to the new fact as best they
could, using the categories and forms of thought that were
available to them. Life and incorruption, not a ready-made
new dogma, were brought to light through the Gospel.

At the centre of the New Testament treatment of our subject stands 1 Corinthians 15, and it is necessary at this stage
to recall the contents of the chapter, though, when I have
brought out some of its themes, I shall return to our sketch
of the development of thought. After that we shall return
(I hope, with profit) to the New Testament.

The centre of Paul's argument is the point that I have already mentioned as essential to the New Testament treatment of our theme: the connexion between Christ's resurrection and ours. He was raised as the first-fruits of all sleepers (1 Cor. 15.20); to deny, as some had done, the possibility of our resurrection was to deny the possibility of Christ's (15.16), and thus to exclude a vital element of the Christian proclamation, in which all preachers were agreed (15.11). If we ask in what the Corinthian error consisted, the answer is probably not an Epicurean denial of all life after death, nor a preference for the immortality of the soul over the resurrection of the body, but the belief (cf. 2 Tim. 2.18, 1 Cor. 4.8) that the resurrection had already, in a spiritual but complete sense, taken place.[9] This view accounts for the fact that Paul devotes a great part of the chapter to straightforward apocalyptic, describing what he expects to take place at the time of the end. This futurist eschatology it was necessary (from Paul's point of view) to ensure. The trumpet shall sound, and the dead shall be raised incorruptible, and we shall be changed (15.52). But this is not the only theme in 1 Corinthians 15. Paul's insistence upon the apocalyptic fulfilment of the work of Christ does not lead him to forget that the decisive work of Christ has already been accomplished. I note here especially the description of Christ as the new Adam (15.21–2, 45), who has become the head of a new humanity. Since by man came death, by man came also the resurrection of the dead; for as in Adam all die, even so in Christ shall all be made alive. As is the heavenly man, so also are (or will be) the heavenly men. Now it must be remembered that Paul understood the inheritance which Adam had handed down to his descendants to be death. Through the sin of that one man death entered into the experience of men (Rom. 5.12); Paul is, of course, dependent on Genesis 2.17. Correspondingly, the inheritance that the new humanity received from the new Adam was life and incorruption; from the heavenly man springs the race of heavenly men. The human race will not reach its goal until Christ has handed over the kingdom to the Father, that God may be all in all (15.24, 28); but already men have moved into the new age ushered in by Christ's resurrection, and their transformation – from glory to glory (2 Cor. 3.18) – has begun.

More light is thrown on Paul's thought by 2 Corinthians 5.1–10, where the same pattern of hope and anticipation recurs, though with perhaps a slightly different balance. The apocalyptic element remains: we must all appear before the judgement seat of Christ (5.10). But it is now more plainly stated that we already have a building from God, a house not made with hands, eternal in the heavens (5.1), which, Paul says with a sharp change of metaphor), we long to put on. It is because of this heavenly dwelling that he can speak of his desire to be absent from the body and present with the Lord (5.8; cf. Phil. 1.23).

Paul's conception of the future life is thus two-fold, as is his conception of (for example) the moral life. Great and decisive things have already been done for men by God in Christ; yet an hour of judgement and of transformation is still to come. This complex doctrine sprang directly out of the person of Jesus himself, recognized by Paul as alive, yet still to be manifested in glory, overcome the last enemy, death (1 Cor. 15.26), and thus complete his work. It is not surprising that it was simplified and distorted by men whose minds were less subtle and profound, and less firmly fixed on Christ, than was Paul's.

It was not long before the vital distinction which Paul draws between body and flesh was overlooked. Already the author of 2 Clement had failed to see the point, and was insisting, as Paul does not, upon the resurrection of the flesh, Let none of you say that this flesh (αὕτη ἡ σάρξ) is not judged or raised up. Understand this. In what were you saved, in what did you recover sight, if it was not when you were in this flesh? We must therefore guard the flesh as God's shrine;

for as you were called in the flesh, so also shall you come in the flesh' (9). A little later Justin makes the same point even more explicitly. There are, he says, men who say that there is no resurrection of the dead, but that immediately upon death their souls are received up into heaven.[10] Do not suppose, Justin goes on, that these men are Christians. They are no more Christians than Sadducees are Jews. All orthodox Christians know that there will be a resurrection of the flesh (σαρκὸς ἀνάστασιν γενήσεσθαι ἐπισταμεθα). Again, it is profitable to trace in the history of the Creeds the development of *resurrectio mortuorum* or *resurrectio corporis* into *resurrectio carnis*, and in due course into *resurrectio carnis hujus*; and I cannot forbear to add the statement of Bachiarius, who in the early fifth century defended his orthodoxy before the Pope in these terms:

> We confess that the flesh of our resurrection is an entire and perfect (resurrection) of this, in which we live in the present age, whether we are governed by good morals or give in to evil works, in order that in it we may be able either to suffer the torments of punishment for evil deeds, or receive the rewards of good things for good deeds. Nor do we say, as some most absurdly do, that another flesh will be raised up instead of this one, but this very flesh, with no member cut off from it nor any other part of the body abandoned.

It is easy to smile at this *naïveté*, but equally it should not be difficult to see the motives that lay behind it. One motive has already been brought out in the quotation from 2 Clement. If you remember that your flesh is to be raised up you will keep it pure. This is very close to Paul's argument in 1 Corinthians 6.13–15, except that Paul speaks not of the flesh but of the body – a distinction which Bachiarius was not alone in failing to grasp. A second motive appears in Ignatius. The resurrection of Jesus was a resurrection of the flesh, a fact which secures (against the Docetists) the reality of his whole fleshly ministry; and it was their conviction of, their actual contact with, his fleshly existence after his resurrection that gave the apostles their confidence and victory in the face of death. That is, they themselves looked forward to a fleshly (as well as spiritual) resurrection, and this hope was linked with a realistic and anti-docetic estimate of the person of Christ himself.[11] Ignatius, indeed, has another interest in this matter, which appears when he describes the bread of the eucharist as the medicine of immortality, the antidote against death (*Ephesians* 20); but to discuss this would take us too far from our main theme.

Among Christians who would otherwise be described as orthodox there is a growing tendency to think of the future life in not merely corporeal but carnal terms. What lies before the Christian is a raising up of the flesh he now has. If he has kept it pure he will be rewarded; if not, in his impure flesh he will suffer.

A second line of development can be traced in early Christian thought, and this too has clearly discernible motivation. We have already heard echoes of it, in (for example) Justin. The trend of gnostic thought was to reject the flesh as intrinsically evil (this incidentally is not really a Greek but an oriental view), and to look forward to its annihilation in death, and to the correspondingly brighter burning of the inward spark of divine life.

At its worst, Christian gnosticism was fundamentally unbiblical speculation destructive alike of Christian faith and Christian morals; but the whole phenomenon of gnosticism cannot be dismissed in these terms, and there are places where it seems to do more justice to the Pauline teaching we have glanced at than do some of the more reputable patristic writers. I propose to illustrate this briefly from some of the recently recovered gnostic texts.

It is characteristic of gnosticism that it individualizes the biblical eschatology. Thus we may compare with the New Testament parable of the Pearl of Great Price the variation, similar in form but decidedly different in emphasis, found in the Gospel of Thomas:

> The kingdom of the Father is like a man, a merchant, who possessing merchandise [and] found a pearl. That merchant was prudent. He sold the merchandise, he bought the one pearl for himself. Do you also seek for the treasure which fails not, which endures, there where no moth comes near to devour and [where] no worm destroys.[12]

Contempt of the flesh appears in Logion 37:

> His disciples said: When wilt thou be revealed to us and when will we see thee? Jesus said: When you take off your clothing without being ashamed, and take your clothes and put them under your feet as the little children and tread on them, then [shall you behold] the Son of the Living (One) and you shall not fear.

This is scarcely a scriptural outlook. But in Logion 51 there is a biblical truth which the Church too often overlooked:

> His disciples said to him: When will the repose of the dead come about and when will the new world come? He said to them: What you expect has come, but you know it not.

This point may be taken farther by means of some quotations from the Gospel of Philip, which calls in question any facile understanding of death and life.

> A Gentile man does not die, for he has never lived that he should die. He who has come to believe in the truth has found life, and this man is in danger of dying, for he is alive since the day Christ came.[13]

Saying 21 makes a similar point with regard to the resurrection of the Lord himself, and Saying 90 returns to the same theme:

> Those who say 'They will die first and rise again' are in

error. If they do not first receive the resurrection while they live, when they die they will receive nothing.

In other words, it is useless simply to look for an act of resurrection in the future; there can be no such act in the future if an act of resurrection has not already taken place. The decisive moment of vivification must take place before death; otherwise there will be nothing to look forward to after death. That this is related to Paul's own belief is clear, but in itself it might be no more than the error contained in the belief of Hymenaeus and Philetus (2 Tim 2.18) that 'the resurrection' had already happened. The question is, what will take place as the third step, after the inauguration of new life, and the death of the body? An answer, obscure and not entirely satisfactory, but with an even clearer Pauline ring, is given in the Gospel of Philip.

> Some are afraid lest they rise naked. Because of this they wish to rise in the flesh, and they do not know that those who bear the flesh [it is they who are] naked; those who... themselves to unclothe themselves [it is they who are] not naked. 'Flesh [and blood shall] not inherit the kingdom [of God].' What is this which will not inherit? This which we have. But what is this which will inherit? That which belongs to Jesus with his blood. Because of this he said: He who shall not eat my flesh and drink my blood has no life in him. What is it? His flesh is the logos, and his blood is the Holy Spirit. He who has received these has food and drink and clothing. For myself, I find fault with the others who say that it will not rise. Then both of these are at fault. Thou sayest that the flesh will not rise; but tell me what will rise, that we may honour thee. Thou sayest the spirit in the flesh, and it is also this light in the flesh. But this too is a logos which is in the flesh, for whatever thou shalt say thou sayest nothing outside the flesh. It is necessary to rise in this flesh, in which everything exists.[14]

The divergence of a gnostic heresy, which nevertheless preserved some of the truths of the New Testament faith, and an anti-gnostic orthodoxy, which nevertheless petrified where it did not deny fundamental Christian conviction, is the great tragedy of the post-apostolic age. It is well illustrated by the particular theme of this lecture. The story I have sketched may be roughly compared to a converging beam of light. A variety of rays, the sombre half-light of Hades and Sheol, the intellectual conception of the immortality of the soul, the often crude notion of reawakened corpses, is brought to a blazing focus, where all half-truths find their full realization, in the resurrection of Jesus. But no sooner is the focus reached than it is passed, and the beam of light fans out again, and not without distortion, so that some confine themselves to a grossly materialist conception of the resurrection of this flesh, others to mystical abstractions or sacramentarian realism. The Christian man who is bereaved of his loved ones, who in the end himself faces the last enemy, can be satisfied with nothing less than the full content of New Testament teaching; and our study has been pure antiquarianism if we are not now prepared to grasp this teaching more firmly and completely.

What we have seen in our historical sketch has been, first, the development among Greeks and Hebrews of a variety of categories in which men's hope for a blessed life after the death of the body could be expressed, and second, the disintegration of the New Testament conviction of the victory of Christ into partial and doctrinaire statements, expressing now one aspect, now another, of a comprehensive belief, according to the taste and preconceived notions of believers. The New Testament (taken as a whole) called on the full range of pre-Christian categories, and needed to do so, because its own conception was many-sided and demanded a wide range of expression. Its writers all accept, and in a variety of ways develop, the fact that Jesus of Nazareth, having truly died, was truly raised from the dead – a fact

84

of history, but a fact without precedent or parallel, and of unique significance in the history of mankind. Equally, they accept, in varying forms, as a fact of the future, that the work of Jesus will be consummated in final victory. The life of Christians is an eschatological existence, totally determined by its position between these two poles, and it follows that, for the individual Christian and for the human race as a whole, the divine gift of life may be viewed under two aspects. God has given life to men, and he will give it; God has raised them from the dead, and he will raise them from the dead. And the gift that has already been given, and the resurrection that has already happened, though not final, are more than metaphorical. If any man is in Christ, there is a new act of creation; old things have passed away, new things have come into being (2 Cor. 5.17).

The New Testament does not borrow precisely the old Jewish conception of the rising up of corpses (though before long, Papias for example, was to do so, in the crudest way imaginable). In a passage we have already studied Paul insists that the resurrected body, though continuous with the natural body, is not identical with it, since it is a spiritual body (1 Cor. 15.44). Similarly the New Testament does not simply reproduce the 'Greek' notion of the immortality of the soul, since it makes clear that what man has inherited from Adam is death. As man and sinner he can expect no other wage. The New Testament writers commit themselves to no ready-made doctrine; but just as, beyond question, they use and adapt the notion of resurrection so also they may be said to use and adapt that of immortality, though the latter is less widespread in the New Testament than, and is secondary to, the former. Man as man is not immortal; neither as man is he assured of resurrection. As Christian, as the new man, he receives a present life that assures him of future life, and a preliminary resurrection that assures him of final resurrection; may we not say, he receives a kind of immortality in the assurance that God will raise him up at the last day? Man may be said to become immortal, not in his own right, as being, or having, a soul, but because God assures him that He will raise him up at the last day. It is this pregnant compound of gift and promise that gnostics and orthodox, from the second century onwards, were to rend in two. It must be remembered that the New Testament itself uses the term immortality, and its near synonym incorruption. Immortality belongs in the first instance to God alone:

> The blessed and only potentate, the king of those who reign as kings and lord of those who exercise lordship, who alone possesses immortality (ἀθανασία), dwelling in light unapproachable, whom no man ever saw, or can see (1 Tim 6.15–16).

But men may seek incorruption (ἀφθαρσία, Rom. 2.7), and God in giving men the Gospel, has brought to light the incorruption they seek (2 Tim. 1.10). The passage in which these words are used most frequently (1 Cor. 15. 42, 50, 52–4) looks unmistakably to the future, to the last day when God will raise the dead in a state of incorruption, and miraculously transform those who still survive. But as we have already seen, we must put 2 Corinthians 5 along with 1 Corinthians 15, not to contradict it but to supplement it, and 2 Corinthians 5.1 speaks of an eternal dwelling already existing in heaven.

The fact that the New Testament hope is thus, in some sense, related both to the idea of personal immortality and to that of resurrection, accounts for the apparent inconsistencies in the Pauline epistles. It has often been pointed out that whereas in 1 Thessalonians 4 and 1 Corinthians 15 Paul draws an apocalyptic picture of a future resurrection, thereby implying that the Christian unfortunate enough to die before the *parousia* can hope for nothing more than sleep in a bodiless nakedness (in Sheol perhaps) until the last day, in 2 Corinthians 5.10 and Philippians 1.23 he implies that death is gain, since immediately the departed Christian is at home with the Lord – which is very far better. It must be granted at once that in these two groups of passages Paul is not saying the same thing. This is because he is applying a rich and diverse doctrine in different directions for different purposes. For the Thessalonians, what really matters is that their dead will not miss the joy of those who survive till the *parousia*. In Corinth, denial of the future aspect of the Christian life had to be countered by its reaffirmation. But elsewhere we find a Christian man face to face with the question: 'What happens next?' And Paul at least is confident that life in the future will mean what life means now – Christ.

A further key to these apparently inconsistent statements is perhaps to be found in the idea of sleep. The significance of this metaphor has been sought by Dr Cullmann (and by Shakespeare before him) in the thought of 'what dreams may come', but it may rather be found in the notion of timelessness. Sleep is essentially timeless. Between the moment of falling asleep and that of waking five minutes or five hours by the clock may intervene, but the sleeper himself passes instantaneously from the one to the other. So after death the intervals of time lose their relevance; for those who are in Christ, there is only a 'for ever with the Lord'. And the Christian may well be thankful for the manifold complexity of his hope. It is not grounded in himself – his intellectual processes, his virtues, or his religious observances – but in God alone. Yet God himself has assured his creatures of the future, first by the resurrection of Jesus Christ, and secondly by implanting in man, in virtue not of his creation but of his redemption, the seed of immortality. But this immortality is not an intellectually and individualistically conceived survival, but a hope that is realized only in the completed people of God in the timeless life beyond the last day.

NOTES

1. Cullmann, op. cit., p. 7.
2. *He That Cometh* (Oxford, 1956), p. 273.
3. I had written this sentence before I saw the Drew Lecture for 1963, and am glad now to be able to appeal to Dr N. H. Snaith's 'Justice and Immortality' (*Scottish Journal of Theology*, XVII. (1964). 309–24).
4. B. Jowett, *The Dialogues of Plato* (Oxford, 1875) i. 423.
5. *Theologisches Wörterbuch zum Neuen Testament*, VI. 377. 46ff.
6. *Bell. Jud.*, ii. 163.
7. S.B. iv. 1017.
8. See M. Black, in *The Background of the New Testament and Its Eschatology* (Cambridge, 1956), p. 175; also *The Scrolls and Christian Origins* (London, 1961), pp. 138f, 190f; and Millar Burrows, *More Light on the Dead Sea Scrolls* (London, 1958), p. 346.
9. See the note by W. G. Kummel in his revised edition (Tübingen, 1949) of Lietzmann's *An die Korinther I, II*, pp. 192f.
10. *Trypho*, 80.
11. See especially *Smyrnaeans* 3.
12. Logion 76.
13. Saying 4.
14. Saying 23.

Just Men Made Perfect

G. B. CAIRD

A child, obviously of Victorian upbringing, once said that he did not want to go to heaven, because that was the place where it was always Sunday. To him Sunday was a privation, an absence of the positive abundance of life which filled his weekday existence. Heaven was therefore reachable but repugnant. This child may perhaps help us to understand why belief in an afterlife has failed to command not so much the faith as the interest of our own generation, to which the present with all its solid achievements seems too vivid to be dismissed as a weary pilgrimage to a better land. At the other extreme there are those to whom heaven seems attractive but unattainable. Heaven is for the good, for those who can claim a first or at least a good second in the final examination, and is therefore as far beyond the reach of us ordinary mortals as the Order of Merit or a gold medal at the Olympic Games.

At a superficial reading the Epistle to the Hebrews appears to lend equal support to each of these antithetical notions. On the one hand it describes the true end of man as a sabbath rest (4.9), lying at the end of a pilgrimage through a world order which possesses only a shadow of the good things to come (10.1), and it urges its readers to emulate the heroes of the past 'for whom this world was not good enough' (11.38). On the other hand it calls the citizens of the heavenly Jerusalem 'just men made perfect' (12.23), it castigates its readers because, unweaned from the milk of an infantile faith, they have failed to grow into the perfect maturity of Christian manhood (5.9ff), and it appears to hold them responsible not only for their own perfection, but for that of past generations as well. 'These also, one and all, are commemorated for their faith; and yet they did not enter upon the promised inheritance, because, with us in mind, God had made a better plan, that only in company with us should they reach their perfection' (11.39f). The Christian athlete is therefore required to run his lap of the relay race before the eyes of an audience with a personal interest in his success, because, if he should stumble or drop the baton, not he alone but the whole team would be the loser. The general neglect of this remarkable epistle is surely due at least as much to the rigour of its demand as to the supposed aridity of its unintelligible and unconvincing argument. As far as I can judge from the list of titles, no lecturer in this series has ever devoted a whole lecture to the Epistle to the Hebrews, and I propose therefore to re-examine the idea of perfection which is its contribution to the New Testament doctrine of immortality.

The author of the epistle sets out to achieve a pastoral purpose by means of an intricate theological argument, and the passage from which the title of this lecture is drawn is both the pastoral and the theological climax of this work. He writes with a passionate concern, which he can barely restrain from irrupting into his discourse, because he is afraid that his friends are in imminent danger of drifting away from a genuine and adult Christian faith. They are, as Alexander Nairne has said, a company of bookish men, converts from Judaism who remain deeply at home in the Old Testament; and the danger to which they are exposed is that they should fail to grasp the full richness of the Christian revelation through a reluctance to cut their ties with a beloved and satisfying past and to go out in faith into the unknown, as once Abraham had done. What they must learn is that no man can be true to the Old Testament who tries to find in it his abiding city. Not only is the Old Testament an incomplete book, it is an avowedly incomplete book, written by men well aware that it was only volume one of the divine revelation, which pointed forward to the day when the God who had spoken in fragmentary and varied fashion through the prophets should speak fully and finally in a Son. This then is the thesis which our author undertakes to prove by a detailed exegesis of his four main scriptural texts.

The incompleteness of the Old Testament is illustrated first by Psalm 8. Our author takes this psalm to mean that in God's design man was intended to live for a short time in subordination to angels, specifically the angels through whom the Mosaic law was given, to whom God had entrusted the authority over that age of world history which was to last until the coming of his Son (2.2, 5), but subsequently to be raised to a glory and honour higher than that of any angel, including authority over the whole subject creation. His first comment is, 'We do not in fact see the whole universe in subjection to man. But we see Jesus . . . crowned through the suffering of death with glory and honour' (2.8f), and in him we see one appointed by God to lead many sons to the glory he himself already enjoys. In other words, the Old Testament presents an ideal of human destiny, which in the nature of things could never be fulfilled as long as man continued to live under the authority of the Old Testament (lower than the angels), but which is now in the process of fulfilment. The second illustration is provided by Psalm 95, which shows that Christ is superior to Moses. Moses faithfully discharged the task that God had given him to do, led Israel out of Egypt, gave them the law, set before them a promise of entering into God's rest; but he was unable to elicit from his own generation a faith which could appropriate the promise, 'the word was not mixed with faith in those who heard it' (4.2). The psalmist, writing many years later, 'Today, if you will listen to his voice', discloses his own belief that the same promise remained at that time outstanding and unfulfilled, and is therefore witness to the superiority of Christ, through whom, as Christian experience attests, men are now able to enter the promised rest. Thirdly, the incompleteness of the Old Testament is shown by Psalm 110. At the heart of Old Testament religion was a priesthood derived from Aaron, whose function it was to offer sacrifices on behalf of the whole nation. The psalmist recognizes the ineffectiveness of these institutions, since otherwise he would not have looked forward to the establishment of a new priesthood in the succession of Melchizedek. Finally, there is Jeremiah with his prophecy of a new covenant, about which our author simply and justifiably remarks: 'When he says "new", he renders the former covenant obsolete, and what is obsolete and ageing is near to disappearance' (8.13). The obsolescence of the old régime does not, of course, mean that the Old Testament was devoid of men with real and effective faith in God. But their faith was in the future. 'Faith gives substance to men's hopes and makes them certain of realities not yet seen' (11.1; cf. 11.7). All the men included in the cavalcade of the faithful lived by confidence in God's future act of grace and declared themselves citizens of a city as yet unbuilt. The Christian Church, by contrast, is able to meet, not under the menacing slopes of Sinai, but in the calm confidence of the heavenly Jerusalem, whose citizens are 'the spirits of just men made perfect'.

The point which concerns us in all this lengthy argument is that perfection is treated throughout not as a human duty or achievement, but as an act of God, belonging only to his full revelation through Christ, and not even contemplated in the preliminary stage of the Old Testament. Four times in as many chapters the writer returns to this same theme. 'If perfection had been attainable through the Levitical priesthood, ... what further need would there have been for the psalmist to speak of another priest arising in the succession of Melchizedek?' (7.11). 'Nothing was brought to perfection by the law, but by the introduction of a better hope, through which we draw near to God' (8.19). 'The offerings and sacrifices there prescribed cannot bring the worshipper to perfection by giving him a clear conscience' (9.9). 'The law contains but a shadow of the good things which were to come; it provides for the same sacrifices year after year, and with these it can never bring the worshippers to perfection for all time' (10.1).

You will notice that the author associates a clear conscience with the idea of perfection. But we must not therefore conclude that perfection is synonymous with moral goodness. For in three other places he speaks of the process by which Christ himself became perfect. 'It was fitting that God, the goal and source of all that is, in bringing many sons to glory, should make the pioneer of their salvation perfect through suffering' (2.10). 'Once perfected he became the source of eternal salvation for all who obey him' (5.9). 'The priest appointed by the oath which supersedes the law is the Son, made perfect for ever' (7.28). It is quite out of the question to interpret these three passages as though they meant that Jesus was at one time morally imperfect and had to be brought to complete goodness by the discipline of God. This author shared the common belief of the New Testament in the sinlessness of Jesus. Jesus was 'dedicated, innocent, undefiled, separated' (7.26). In his case at least therefore perfection implies some other form of growth to completeness.

The first of the three passages is concerned with Jesus as the fulfilment of human destiny. Man was destined by God for glory and honour beyond that accorded to the angels, and Jesus has now not only attained to that glory himself, but has become the Saviour, capable of leading many sons to glory. But in order to be this, he had to share to the utmost all the conditions of human life. He must leave no human experience unexplored, and in particular he must fathom the very depths of temptation. Only if it can truly be said that

> Christ leads me through no darker rooms
> Than he went through before,

is he fully equipped to be the pioneer of man's salvation. He must be at every point put on a level with those he is to address as brothers. The sufferings he underwent are a part of that identification, and it is in this sense that he is said to be made 'perfect through suffering'. He is thus completely qualified for his calling.

But this is not the whole meaning. He is called pioneer, the trail-blazer who opens up a new path along which others can follow him. But in that case all his achievements must be such as are open to them also. He must not rely on powers on which they cannot draw. 'He who consecrates and they who are consecrated are all of one' (2.11); and he must derive his sanctity from the same source as they. Like them, he must live by faith and prayer. This point is further developed in the second of our passages. 'In the days of his earthly life he offered up prayers and petitions, with loud cries and tears, to God who was able to save him from death; and in the midst of his fear his prayer was heard. Son though he was, he learned obedience in the school of suffering, and, once perfected, became the source of eternal salvation to all who obey him' (5.7–9). Let me repeat, there is no question here of Jesus being at one time disobedient and having to learn to obey. From start to finish he was obedient. But he had to learn by personal experience what obedience involved, where in this dark world obedience would lead; and he could do this only because he was content to live by faith and to leave results in the hands of God. Even in the face of the horror and bewilderment of Gethsemane he must walk by faith. He is said to be perfected because he followed to the end the road of faith and obedience, though it led him into the uttermost depths of human darkness. All his victories were won, not by some innate power, but by faith in God; and it is this that has made him the pioneer of our faith (12.2). He is not only a man who has shared our manhood, but the most fully human person who has ever lived.

But still the most important thing remains to be said. This Jesus through death has passed into the inner presence of God, and has done this too as pioneer, in such a way that others may follow. In the central chapters of the epistle a contrast is drawn between the Levitical priesthood and the priesthood of Christ. In the earthly temple the presence of God was symbolized by the holy of holies, into which no man ever went except the high priest, and he only on one day of the year, the Day of Atonement. Our author takes this to mean that, as long as the earthly temple was the centre of religion, the way to God for the ordinary worshipper was barricaded, not indeed by the rules of temple ritual, but by the sin of which those rules were a reminder. This is the real heart of his meaning when he says that 'nothing was brought to perfection by the law'. For man's perfection is achieved precisely when he stands in the presence of his Maker. But Christ has entered into the heavenly sanctuary, of which the earthly temple was but a copy and a shadow, and by his sacrifice of obedience has so dealt with sin that the humblest believer may follow along the new and living way which he opened up.

We are now in a position to sum up what was involved in the perfecting of Christ and what is the perfection that he opens up for others. He himself was made perfect because he experienced to the full all the conditions of human life, because by a faith and obedience, a dependence on God which is open to all men to share, he won the right to enter God's presence, and won it not for himself alone but for all who were prepared to let him call them brothers. The citizens of the heavenly Jerusalem can be called just men made perfect for no other reason than that they have been admitted to the presence of God. The reason no man was ever brought to perfection by the law or the old covenant was that under the old covenant it was thought that man must be morally fit to enter the divine presence: he must have clean hands and a pure heart. The new covenant is more realistic. It recognizes that God himself is the only source of goodness and holiness, that only through vital contact with him can man become good and holy. Moral goodness is the consequence, not the precondition, of access to God.

Up to this point we have been following the clue of perfection as it threads its way through the thought of the epistle. Now we discover that, intertwined with it so closely as to form almost a single strand, is another thread, the thread of access or approach. 'Since therefore we have a great high priest who has passed through the heavens ... let us boldly approach the throne of our gracious God' (4.14–16). 'Nothing was brought to perfection by the law, but by the introduction of a better hope, by which we draw near to God' (7.19). 'He is able to save absolutely those who approach God through him' (7.25). 'The law ... cannot bring to perfection for all time those who approach God' (10.1). 'The blood of Jesus makes us free to enter boldly into the sanctuary by the new, living way he has opened for us ... so let us make our approach in sincerity of heart and full assurance of faith' (10.22). 'You have not made your approach to the palpable, blazing fire of Sinai ... you have made your approach to Mount Sion, and the city of the living God' (12.18, 22). The right of approach to the throne of our gracious God is the one perfection which carries with it all else that men can hope or desire. Amongst other things it carries with it, as we shall see, eternal life. Yet in the thinking of this author this is almost coincidental: what matters is not that we should live for ever, but that we should live with God.

It may be worth while to interject at this point a few words about the sacrificial imagery which plays so large a part in the language of this epistle, because this is one of the reasons that make it so foreign to the modern mind. The New Testament uses many kinds of picture to illustrate its doctrine of salvation. When it speaks of justification, it draws its picture from the lawcourt; when it speaks of victory, from the battlefield; when it speaks of redemption, from the slave-market. All this imagery is meaningful to us because we still have our lawcourts, battlefields, prisons and concentration-camps. But the practice of ritual sacrifice is no part of our modern experience, and imagery drawn from this source tends to leave our imaginations untouched. But in this way we are in danger of losing a very important part of the message of the New Testament. For each of these pictures corresponds to a different aspect of sin. If salvation is described as justification, then sin is being treated as guilt, with an emphasis on the responsibility of the sinner. If salvation is described as redemption, then sin is conceived as a bondage from which man cannot fight his way free. But if salvation is described in the language of sacrifice, then sin is regarded as a taint or uncleanness. The idea of moral evil as dirt, which disqualifies a person from the company of God or man, lies very deep in the psychology of the human race. The Old Testament emphasis on uncleanliness may strike us as a singularly undiscriminating one, but it was a reminder to men that there were elements in their common life which disqualified them from access to God. And this is surely the deepest level at which we can face the reality of sin. What the Epistle to the Hebrews asserts is that this barrier between man and God has been transcended, not by man's penitence or reformation, but by God's descent. Christ has become totally like, totally indentified with his human brothers, bound to them by a tie of sympathy so complete and so permanent that they remain united with him when he enters the heavenly sanctuary.

The language of sacrifice and access is not, however, the only means used in this epistle to define the perfection to which the Christian is called. There are three other images which help to fill out the picture of the eternal life which begins now and continues hereafter. The first is the image of the sabbath rest, to which I alluded in my opening words. The word *sabbatismos* occurs in the course of the author's exposition of Psalm 95. The psalmist had called on his own contemporaries to listen to the voice of God and accept God's promise of rest, unlike Moses' generation who had lost their

opportunity through unbelief. But what did the psalmist
mean by 'God's rest'? He cannot have meant the end of the
wilderness wanderings and settlement in an earthly home,
because, though Moses failed in this respect, Joshua succeeded; and the psalmist speaks as though God's promise
were still unfulfilled. He must therefore have had in mind a
heavenly rest. At this point in his argument our author iden-
tifies the *katapausis* (which is the Greek word for rest used
in the Septuagint version of the psalm) with another kind
of rest, the *sabbatismos* or sabbath rest into which God is said
to have entered on the seventh day of creation. In other
words, the rest which is offered to men is not merely a rest
which God gives; it is the very rest which God himself enjoys.
We are here very far away from the childish distaste for a
heaven where it is always Sunday. We need not entertain
extravagant notions of God fretfully trying to while away the
interminable hours of a wet Victorian sabbath. God's *sabbatismos* is the rest not of inertia, idleness and negation, but of
positive attainment and fruition. There may be fields of
human experience where Stevenson's dictum holds good,
that 'to travel hopefully is a better thing than to arrive', but
there are certainly exceptions. It is not obviously better for
the youthful pianist, let alone for those who must listen to
him, to travel hopefully at his practice than to arrive at the
capacity to play the Hammerklavier Sonata. There are many
forms of enjoyment no less active, and certainly no less satisfying, than the laboursome process which made them possible.
But the Christian who enters into rest does something more
than enjoy the fruits of his labours. He is admitted to the
joy with which the Creator himself regards the products of
his own artistry and love.

From this we must now turn to the second image of heaven
as a city. Abraham, we are told, even after his arrival in
Canaan, refused to regard this as journey's end. His earthly
travels to an earthly destination were but the symbol of
another journey. He therefore continued to live in tents,

refusing to find in this transient existence a permanent home; 'for he was looking forward to the city with firm foundations, whose architect and builder is God' (11.10). And again: 'God is not ashamed to be called their God; for he has a city ready for them' (11.16). I suppose the first deduction to be made from these citations is that the author of Hebrews believed in what the hymn calls 'social joys'. All that I have said about access to the presence of God might conceivably be taken to mean that salvation and the eternal life that issues from it are essentially individual experiences, an I-Thou relationship with the Almighty. (I cannot, by the way, understand the remarkable popularity among theologians of that singularly unchristian phrase. Surely the New Testament teaches us that even in solitary prayer the Christian ought to use the first person *plural* in his address to God.) Whatever individualism we may have inherited from the Age of Reason, this epistle has little room for it. The promise of sabbath rest is made to 'the people of God', and here as elsewhere in the New Testament heaven is pictured as a city. In the Pauline theology eternal life could hardly be other than corporate, since it is made possible only by incorporation into the body of Christ. Our author thinks rather of a family solidarity, established by that sympathy which prompted Christ to call men his brothers, but his idea of immortality is no less corporate than that of Paul.

At this point we encounter one of the most popular misconceptions about the Epistle to the Hebrews. The author declares in one place that the earthly temple was only a shadowy copy of the perfect heavenly temple which Moses had seen on Mount Sinai, and in another that the law with all its religious ordinances possessed only 'a shadow of the good things that were to come' (8.5; 10.1). It has therefore been assumed that he was imbued with a Platonic world view, in which all earthly objects are but copies and shadows of the perfect patterns laid up in heaven. According to this view Abraham's faith consisted in his refusal to be satisfied with the realm of things seen and temporal, and the city to which he aspired was one not of this world. But this interpretation makes nonsense of the sentence which concludes the catalogue of the faithful heroes of the Old Testament: 'these also, one and all, are commemorated for their faith; and yet they did not enter upon the promised inheritance, because, with us in mind, God had made a better plan, that only in company with us should they reach their perfection' (11.39f). They died without having entered the promised land! But how could it be otherwise, if the promised land lay beyond the river of death? And what would then be the point of saying that God had a better plan in store for us?

The answer to these questions, as C. K. Barrett has clearly demonstrated in his contribution to the *Festschrift* in honour of C. H. Dodd, is that the two worlds of this epistle are not those of Platonic idealism; they are the two worlds of Jewish eschatology, the one following upon the other in historic sequence. The realm of shadow and transience is not here the whole phenomenal world, it is the world of the Old Testament, declared by its own prophetic writers to be obsolescent and near to disappearing. And the real world of which it was a shadowy anticipation is the new age introduced by Christ. The glory and honour with which Christ was crowned are the tokens of his authority over the world to come, which takes on a present reality in his person (2.5ff.). Christians are accordingly those who have 'tasted the goodness of God's gift and the powers of the age to come' (6.5). This explains why it can be said that God had a better plan in store for Christians. To Abraham the city of God was only a vision of God's future, to which he clung in faith; but to the Christian it is a present fact. 'You have come to Mount Sion and the city of the living God' (12.22). Christ has opened up a new and living way into God's presence and therefore into God's city. This is why Abraham and the rest could reach their perfection only in company with the writer of Hebrews and his fellow-Christians: in them, provided they

G. B. Caird

held fast to their faith, the city of God had ceased to be wholly a vision of the future and had become, in part at least, a fact of the present.

To say all this is not to deny that the city of God is essentially a heavenly and eternal city, but it is a city which is related in a very intimate and special way to the world of earth and time. The city is but another name for the new order which has already supervened upon the old, not by way of negation or contradiction, but gathering up the past with all its shadowy anticipations into the final perfect consummation. The revelation which God gave to the fathers through the prophets in varied and fragmentary fashion has come to full expression in his Son; Christ has carried his own manhood, with all its inherent weakness, with him into the eternal order; the one perfect sacrifice of Christ helps us to see at last what earlier generations were groping after as they offered their bulls and goats, and the recipients of the letter are urged to move boldly out from the security of a well-loved past, in confidence that they will receive it back from God by a better resurrection.

This brings me to my third and final picture, the picture of the great earthquake. This cosmic earthquake is one of the commonest features in the Old Testament expectations of the Day of the Lord. What the origins of this symbol were does not here concern us. Our concern is only with the use to which our author puts it. 'Then (i.e. at Sinai) his voice shook the earth, but now he has promised, "Once more and once only I will shake not earth alone but the heavens also." The words "once more and once only" imply the removal of what is shaken, inasmuch as they are created things, in order that what is not shaken may remain. The kingdom we are given is unshakeable: let us therefore give thanks to God' (12.26ff.). The point of this passage is not that all created things are transient, and that only the uncreated will ultimately survive; for how could men then expect to enter eternity? Christians, transient creatures that they are, have

101

been given an unshakeable kingdom, and they may therefore hope to survive the testing earthquake. In the midst of time they have been touched with eternity. In the person of Jesus they have come into contact with 'the power of an indissoluble life' (7.16). It follows therefore that whatever in the history of man has been touched by the divine presence has thereby been taken out of the category of mere creatureliness to join the ranks of the unshakeable.

This conclusion is borne out by an observation about the typology of this epistle. Christ as high priest corresponds typologically to the priesthood of the Old Testament. What is not commonly recognized is that Christ is prefigured by two types, not one alone. There is Aaron, but there is also Melchizedek; and our author has two different words to distinguish their different relationship to Christ. Aaron and the whole system he administers is a shadow (*skia*) of the good things to come. Melchizedek provides a likeness (*homoiotes*) and he is said to be 'conformed to the Son of God' (7.3). The one possesses the form of priesthood without the effective substance, the other a genuine anticipation of the real thing. In the dawn of Israel's history Melchizedek really did stand on Abraham's Godward side, and through him Abraham really drew near to God. Nor does Melchizedek stand alone in the Old Testament. Whenever there were men of faith, finding no abiding city in the present order but trusting in God's future, there too was a *homoiotes* – a genuine anticipation of Christ. For faith is to be defined as the real grasping of the objects of men's hopes. Wherever there is faith there is a likeness to the Son of God; and wherever there is a likeness to the Son of God, there too is something that cannot be shaken, something which belongs to the ultimate and heavenly city. This is God's better plan, that only in company with those who have accepted Christ on earth should the past find the fulfilment of its hopes and aspirations.

Immortality, then, in the view of this writer, is not a quality inherent in the nature of man, nor even a prize bestowed by God on those who qualify for it. It is an attribute of God himself, which he imparts to those who approach him in the confidence that he is the rewarder of all who seek him. And if this writer seems at times to be harsh in the rigour of his warnings against apostasy and lapse, against drifting away from the living God, this is only because he himself has tasted the goodness of God's gift and the powers of the age to come, and he cannot for a moment imagine where else a man might turn if he chooses to shut his ears to the voice that speaks from heaven, to 'the mediator of the new covenant whose sprinkled blood has better things to say than the blood of Abel' (12.24).

The Contribution of the Book of Revelation to the Christian Belief in Immortality

G. R. BEASLEY-MURRAY

Before we embark on this subject it will be well to review some preliminary considerations relating to the nature of the book of Revelation.

The first is a reminder that although the last book of the Bible deals with the last things of time and history, it is not a dissertation on personal immortality. It is not indeed a dissertation about anything, but rather, as E. F. Scott has expressed it, 'a trumpet call to faith'. In harmony with the emphasis which prevails throughout the Bible, the writer is less concerned with the destiny of the individual than with the future of the Kingdom of God and the world in relation to it. Moreover he understood as fully as any other biblical writer that the Kingdom of God is the rule of God – more precisely, that it is God revealing his sovereignty in deeds of judgement and redemption. If therefore the Revelation is rightly viewed as a book about the Kingdom of God, that means that it is a book about God, who sovereignly brings to pass his purposes of good for the world through Jesus the Christ.

The recognition that the Revelation is a trumpet call to faith rather than a thesis does not have the corollary that it is addressed to the emotions and is devoid of intellectual content, or that it was hastily put together to combat a crisis anticipated in a week's time. On the contrary no book of the Bible has been more carefully or more elaborately constructed than this book. The adoption of the form of an epistle for it enables the writer to establish a rapport with his readers, and their situation is constantly in mind. His opening account of a vision of Christ, commissioning him to prophesy, is followed by the Seven Letters to the Churches. These letters are models of conciseness and precision; in each case the introduction is related to the opening vision of Christ, and the conclusion is related to the vision of the Kingdom recounted at the end of the book. The twofold vision of God and Christ in chapters 4 and 5 forms the fulcrum of the book; it gives the message of the book *in nuce*, and out of it flow the visions of judgements which precede the revelation of the victorious Kingdom. These descriptions of judgement are neither mindless nor heartless repetitions of a process of grinding the wicked world to dust, as some appear to believe. They are an extraordinary elaboration from three different points of view of the traditional messianic woes, each series embodying the principle enunciated in Leviticus 26, 'I will multiply your calamities seven times, as your sins deserve' (vv. 18, 21, 24, 28).

The first series results from the opening of God's book of destiny, which contains his testament or covenant to bestow the Kingdom; the second employs the figure of trumpets which announce the coming of God's new world; the third is presented under the figure of cups of wrath which the world is made to drink. Each series leads up to the point when the Kingdom should be unveiled, but the final revelation is delayed in order that the reader may understand other aspects of the last days which the Church and the world must experience. In particular the central chapters 12–14, coming after the sounding of the last trumpet which heralds the Kingdom of God, set the struggle of the Church and Empire in the context of universal history and the contest of the powers of darkness against the God of light. Similarly after the completion of the cups of wrath, the final chapter of the story again is held up in order to show the reader how the godless empire comes to its end (chs. 17–19). Not till these elements of the picture have been filled in are we permitted to learn the nature of Christ's coming and of the Kingdom which embraces heaven and earth, and history and eternity. Such a brief review conveys little idea of the intricacies of the composition of the Revelation and the compression of biblical, Judaic and other religious traditions in its cameos of judgement and salvation. The more one studies this book the greater is one's astonishment at the artistry of the author and the power of his representations.

A brief comment should be included on the prophet's use of symbolism. Everybody knows that the book of Revelation is full of symbolic pictures. This, together with its preoccupation with the future, is at least part of the reason for its fascination over people through the centuries, but it has enabled many to read in the book just what they wanted. Only in comparatively recent times have we come to appreciate that John's symbolism was neither arbitrary nor invented by him, but constituted a language drawn from an ancient tradition which yet spoke eloquently to his contemporaries. The closest parallel to this mode of communication I can think of is the modern political cartoon which is employed in the newspapers of most countries of the world and in a virtually universally understood language. Cartoons generally purport to convey a message relating to immediate situations, whether of the cartoonist's own locality, or of his country, or of his country's relations to other lands, and sometimes even to what is happening in areas of no immediate concern to him. Many of the pictures used by the cartoonists are stereotyped by long usage, e.g. the figures of Uncle Sam and John Bull, or the Russian Bear, the British Lion, the American Eagle, the Chinese Dragon. Events like the table-tennis matches between the Americans and the Chinese give wonderful opportunities to cartoonists to exploit their ingenuity, and grimmer situations like the Vietnam war or the Middle East conflict are constantly kept under review by them.

Jewish apocalyptists had a veritable art gallery of well-known images from which to draw in their portrayals of the future. The most famous cartoon strip of all was the ancient myth of the sea monster which defied the powers of heaven but was finally subdued by a champion of the gods. Circulating throughout the middle east this story was adapted by Israel's prophets and poets in a variety of ways, and in due time the monster became a standing symbol for evil political powers – hence its employment in the book of Daniel (ch. 7). Its application in this way implied both a judgement on the nature of the power and a prophecy of its sure fate at the hands of God. Hence John utilizes the figure to represent the empire of his day, the antichristian emperor, and the devil who inspires both. Other symbols have a happier history and significance. The myth of the Child Redeemer, who is rescued from the claws of the dragon and becomes its conqueror (ch. 12), is used by John to proclaim the fulfilment by the crucified and risen Christ of the hopes of the world and to rebut claims made on behalf of all other world redeemers. We shall find similarly that the closing vision of the consummated Kingdom in Revelation 21–22 lays under contribution both biblical prophetic traditions and expectations of other religions, and proclaims their fulfilment in the Kingdom of Christ and of God. If the precise meaning of some of the symbols at times is beyond us, we can usually glean the general import of what they are intended to convey.

My final preliminary consideration is perhaps the most important. Our subject is not simply the teaching of the book of Revelation on immortality, but its contribution to the Christian belief in immortality. The question must be faced: Is the book of Revelation Christian? It is, of course, in the canon of the New Testament, but its right to that place was opposed both in the early centuries and in Reformation times, and it has been questioned with renewed vigour in modern times. Some of the greatest contemporary New

Testament scholars have expressed their doubts about the Christian content of the Revelation, believing it to be more Jewish than Christian. Where scholars divide one has to make one's own decision and maintain it with respect for the opinions of others. So far as I am concerned I judge the Book of Revelation to be as Jewish as Jesus and as Christian as Paul. Those who have judged adversely the Book of Revelation have tended to under-estimate the Jewishness of Jesus and the significance of Paul's eschatology. From first line to the last line the Revelation is dominated by the concept of God revealed in the crucified and risen Christ. No book of the New Testament, including the Fourth Gospel and the Letter to the Hebrews, has a higher Christology than that in the Revelation. The Kingdom which is awaited is not simply the Kingdom looked for by the Old Testament prophets, but the Kingdom which has come in the incarnation, death and resurrection of Jesus the Christ and which is to be manifested in his parousia. The tension of the now and not yet of the eschatological teaching of Jesus is translated in the Revelation, in the light of the Easter event, into a unitary activity of the Redeemer in whom the Kingdom has come and is coming. This is observable especially in the crucial vision of chapters 4–5, the theme of which is that the God of creation is the God of redemption, accomplishing his gracious will through the crucified and risen Christ. By his death and resurrection the Lamb of God has 'conquered' so as to open the book of destiny and carry out its prescripts. Whether or not John consciously applies to Christ the idea of the ancient enthronement ceremony to depict his ascent to the throne of the universe, his meaning is unmistakable: he declares that the victory of Christ has already taken place in his Cross and Resurrection, that he has ascended the throne of God, and his reign has begun. The exaltation lies in the past, the acclamation of the hosts of heaven has been given, the acknowledgement rendered by the whole creation lies in the future, but the vision is unbroken. The later chapters of the Revelation show that a special exercise of the divine sovereignty must take place before all rebellion is subdued and the entire universe acclaims its Lord, but this will be the outworking of the central action of the vision. The messianic judgements and the parousia are the closing acts of the Easter drama. This concentration on the great redemptive acts enables us to see that the victory of God in Christ is one, and that it has been won. Only a Christian prophet could so write, and this central vision of his is an epitome of Christian theology. There is good reason to maintain that the rest of the Revelation is a legitimate development of that theology.

John's thought about the destiny of man is most fully expressed in his climactic vision of the City of God, the new Jerusalem (chs. 21–22). It is characteristic of John's visions that in this, his most extensive description of the Kingdom of God, he should combine features drawn from the Old Testament, from Jewish apocalyptic writings and from pagan myths, and complete and correct them all in the light of God's redemption in Christ Jesus. The concept of the city of the gods in heaven was popularized through the Babylonians, and many of the features in John's description may be traced back to such an origin: the twelve gates of the city with their twelve angels may be related to the twelve figures and divisions of the heaven in the Zodiac; the city's precious stones may go back to the shining stars of heaven; the river running through its street, and possibly the street itself, are reminiscent of the Milky Way; the wall of jasper may be suggested by the night horizon; the four-square shape of the city could have been determined by four corners on which the vault of heaven rests. With this concept of the heavenly city is related the myth of the 'mountain of God' (Ezek. 28.16), 'the mountain where the gods meet' (Isa. 14.13) in the north, where the starry constellations revolve. We find in both Isaiah 14 and Ezekiel 28 reflections of the mythical tale of the attempt by the morning star to scale the mountain and thereby become king of the stars, and this passage in Ezekiel is one of the sources used by John for his account of the city of God. Naturally John will also have considered the numerous passages in the Old Testament prophets which speak of the glory of Zion in the age to come, and he further pondered the Genesis account of the paradise in Eden as a picture of the paradise regained in the Kingdom of God.

John's use of these sources is akin to the builder's use of quarries for the edifice he wishes to construct: the stones are taken from them, but the finished product is vastly different from their original context. In truth the hope of Israel is fulfilled in the new Jerusalem, and so also is the pagans' dream of a city in the heavens. But the pagans must learn that the home of the gods is none other than the dwelling of the Father of our Lord Jesus Christ. Its gates are inscribed not with the figures of the Zodiac, but with the names of the tribes of Israel. Its foundations bear the names of the apostles of the Lamb, whose witness is directed to the Christ as the sole redeemer of the world. The stones of which the foundations are made merit special attention, for they are twelve enormous jewels. We learn that they are identical with those on the high priest's breastplate, but more strikingly they also appear to have symbolized in ancient times the twelve divisions of the Zodiac. Charles' demonstration seems to be incontrovertible that John's order of enumerating the city's twelve foundation stones is precisely the reverse order of the progress of the sun through the divisions of the Zodiac. Charles deduced from this that John was anxious to demonstrate that the real city of God had nothing to do with the pagans' city of gods. Perhaps it would be better to interpret John as indicating that the reality for which the pagans looked is not to be found in heathen astrological religion but in the revelation of God in Christ. Accordingly John makes the extraordinary equation of the city of God with the Bride, the Wife of the Lamb. This is not intended to be a simple identification of the Church of Christ with the Kingdom of Christ, for the city is the goal of the Church's pilgrimage;

rather the city denotes the context of the Church's existence in God's new creative activity in Christ. But the interchange of the City and Bride indicates that the ultimate reality in view is people in fellowship with God through Christ. All the categories of salvation are variations on the theme of the restored relation between God and man, and the city of God provides the crown of them all. It comes down from God out of heaven, for only he can provide the context of this perfected fellowship. But this is good news for pagans. For the city which comes down from heaven is not reserved for the gods in the skies, but is prepared for the multitudes of sinful men and women for whom the Redeemer was born, and for whom he lived and died and rose. It is the Kingdom of heaven opened for mankind.

The detailed descriptions of the city therefore illustrate the blessedness of the relationship of God to man in this holy and happy fellowship restored in and through the Redeemer. They are fittingly summed up in the opening and closing paragraphs of the vision: 'Now at last God has his dwelling among men! He will dwell with them and they shall be his people, and God himself will be with them' (21.3); and again, 'The throne of God and of the Lamb will be there, and his servants shall worship him; they shall see him face to face...' (22.3f). The essential feature of the city is that God and the Lamb are there – we recall the closing words of Ezekiel: 'The city's name for ever after shall be Jehovah-Shammah, *the Lord is there.*' But for John 'there' means with his people, hence the name Emmanuel reaches its final fulfilment: he who was with us as the Incarnate in Nazareth is eternally with us in the city.

The very structure of the city embodies this characteristic of its life. It is built as a square, or more precisely as a cube, since its height is the same as its length and breadth. There is little doubt what building John had in mind in so describing it: it was the 'holy of holies', or the inner shrine of the Temple. The city is one vast sacred shrine for the presence of God. But this signifies God's presence with man, not removal from him. We recall that the high priest alone entered Israel's most holy place, and that was but once a year (for some high priests it was but once in a lifetime); in the city which descends from heaven man does not visit God, but dwells with him in freedom. The city therefore has no temple; it is all temple.

And what of its size? 'Twelve thousand furlongs' is the angel's measurement. Moffatt's translation of that into 1500 miles is a mistake, for we have to think of 12 expanded to infinity; nevertheless Moffatt's rendering serves a purpose by reminding us of the dizzy height of the city's sky-scrapers. Perhaps this is the one passage in literature where that term 'sky-scraper' is fitting; for that indicates exactly what the city is intended to do, namely reach from earth to heaven and unite them into one. More than one rabbi tried to express the same thought, as e.g. in the saying that Jerusalem would be enlarged till it reached the gates of Damascus, and exalted till it reached the throne of God. Heaven and earth come together in the city.

Even the substance of the city reflects the nature of God, for its wall is built of jasper, and jasper is named by John as akin to the appearance which he saw in his vision of God on his throne (4.3). No wonder the city has no need of sun or moon or light of man's devising, for 'the glory of God is its light, and its lamp is the Lamb' (21.23); and of course there can be no night there, for the glory of God never dims.

The city has a wall, for in ancient society a wall was constitutive of a city; it kept undesirables out and kept those within safe. The figure of 144 cubits for the height of the wall is impressive, until one thinks of its relation to the city's height, and then it appears absurdly small. But such a wall is enough for its purposes; the city's inhabitants are eternally secure within its walls, and those without cannot scale it. Judgement and mercy unite in the city, as they do at the cross of Jesus.

Nevertheless the city's wall is broken by gates – twelve of

them, three on each side. They are perpetually open – every day and all the day, for there is no night there. And they are constantly used! 'By its light shall the nations walk, and the kings of the earth shall bring into it all their splendour' (21.24), which suggests that nations as well as kings go through the gates. Yet it is also said, 'Nothing unclean shall enter, nor anyone whose ways are false or foul, but only those who are inscribed in the Lamb's roll of the living' (21.27). If the two pictures are put together, and compared with the situation earlier depicted in the Revelation, where the kings of the earth oppose the Church and fight the Lamb, it would appear that some major conversion work has gone on to change the situation so radically. The vision reflects hope on a large scale for a world which has bitterly resisted its Lord and Redeemer.

The city, like Eden, has a river, and it flows down the midst of the city's street. In eastern parlance fresh flowing water is living water, in distinction from static water, as in a pool. The term readily lent itself to a symbolic application for the gift of life itself. Ezekiel, in his vision of the new city and temple, applied it to the river which took its rise from the temple in Jerusalem (47.1ff). John has to modify this, for the city is all temple; the river therefore flows from the throne of God and the Lamb (22.2). We recollect the call of the Christ in John 7.37ff, that the thirsty come to him for drink; this is said in the light of the Scripture, 'Out of that man's body will flow rivers of living water': the living water of Ezekiel's prophecy thus proceeds from the Christ; the Evangelist adds that it comes through the Holy Spirit whom the glorified Christ sends. The pictures in the Gospel and the Revelation are essentially one: the river 'symbolizes the fulness of the life-powers which flow through paradise' (Rissi), and these come through the Spirit whom the Redeemer sends with the dawn of the new age.

The same basic idea is contained in the representation of the tree, or rather trees of life on the river's banks, which yield a crop every month (22.2). Abundance of life for the city's inhabitants again is in view, but an additional thought is appended: 'the leaves of the trees serve for the healing of the nations'; i.e. the ravages and hurt of sin find their balm through the gracious provision of God and the Lamb. Hence 'every accursed thing shall disappear'. The end of paradise lost is the beginning of paradise regained. Light and life prevail in the new order, for the throne of God and the Lamb is unreservedly acknowledged. So surely as the throne stands supreme in the city, so too God's people 'shall reign for ever and ever' (22.5). The summit of the divine purpose therefore is reached; God's people acknowledge his rule, and they share it with him. The love that overflows for man is reciprocated in a love which responds in freedom to God.

John's account of the city of God, as we saw, is a vision of the Kingdom of God in terms of redeemed community in relation to God in Christ. Its primary concern is God's purpose for the race of man, just as the preceding visions of God's judgements have in view the destiny of the nations in the climax of history. Accordingly it is mankind in its major groupings that is in mind rather than individuals. But groups are made up of individuals, as John knows well. If the city of God provides the context of life for renewed humanity, it provides the context of life for the individual member of the renewed race. That John would have us interpret his vision of the Kingdom of God in terms of individual destiny is indicated by the promises to the conquerors which he records at the end of each of the Letters to the Seven Churches. Every one of these letters is addressed to a single congregation, each is applied to the seven churches of Asia Minor, and through them they are addressed to the Church of Christ throughout the world. Yet every letter ends with a promise addressed to the individual member of each congregation, and each promise relates to the blessings to be bestowed in the Kingdom of God, described in the closing vision of the Revelation.

It is strictly irrelevant to our major concern to determine who the conquerors are, whether they are viewed by John as Christ's faithful witnesses who lay down their lives for his sake, i.e. the martyrs, or whether they are Christians who maintain faith and obedience to Christ, come what may. It so happens that a definition of the victor is given in the Letter to Thyatira, namely as 'he who perseveres in doing my will to the end' (2.26). In my view the promises to the conquerors are assurances to the faithful of the benefits of Christ's redemption, expressed in apocalyptic categories and language. In the nature of the case they afford inspiration for faith and fortitude in all who may be called to lay down their lives for Christ, but all believers need such assurances for the whole Church faces a period of severe testing. The letters themselves allow neither the view that all who belong to the Church must die before the end, nor that participation in the city of God is restricted to a group of believers within the Church. The only reason why any believer can be envisaged as a conqueror is because the Christ himself has overcome the world and all evil powers, and he gives his followers to share in his victory. The essential characteristic of the conqueror therefore is that he participates in Christ's conquest through faith, and through persistence in faith he continues to share in Christ's victory to the end, whether the end for him be death or the parousia of Christ.

He who by faith shares in Christ's victory shares in Christ's Kingdom. The promises to the conquerors spell out what this will mean for the individual faithful Christian. For example, the first declares, 'I will grant (him) to eat of the tree of life, which is in the paradise of God' (2.7). That which was forbidden to man in the Garden, and which he forfeited for ever, is therefore the first blessing promised, namely, life eternal. The fruits of the tree add the further thought that life in Christ's Kingdom is characterized by the delights of salvation and fellowship with God and the Lamb and his people.

The second promise repeats the first under different

figures, first positively and then negatively: he who remains faithful will receive 'the crown of life', i.e. the victor's crown after winning the contest; this is no fading wreath of laurel but the gift of incorruptible life. And 'he who conquers shall not be hurt by the second death', i.e. he will not suffer judgement in the world to come. This is the doctrine of justification by faith translated into apocalyptic imagery. Its pertinence to the persecuted church at Smyrna would have been clear: to suffer the wrath of godless man is small compared with the prospect of suffering the judgement of God.

The third promise is complex: the conqueror will be given the hidden manna, a white stone, and a new name which none but he knows. The first element is a variation on the fruit of the tree of life; it reflects the Jewish expectation of the return of the manna in the time of the Kingdom. The white stone could reflect the custom of presenting such a stone to a man after trial, signifying his acquittal, or it could be a counterpart of the ancient ticket of admission to public festivals – in this case to the messianic feast. The new name could be that of the believer himself, who by resurrection has entered on a new status with a unique relation to his Lord; or it could be that of Christ or God, symbolizing the transcendent divine powers placed in his hand but which, being unknown to others, imply a unique role for the believer in the Kingdom of God. Whatever the precise meaning, its importance lies in its illustration that in the age to come the individual continues to matter to God; he sustains a unique relation to God and has his own part to play in God's eternal world.

The fourth promise appears to convey two privileges, but they may be two ways of expressing a single reality; these are authority with Christ over the nations, and the gift of the morning star (2.26ff.). It is likely that the latter is to be interpreted in the light of 1.20, where the seven stars in Christ's hand represent the sovereignty over the world which Christ has bestowed on his churches. The morning star is

Venus, and from ancient times this star served as a symbol of victory and sovereignty – Roman generals erected temples in honour of Venus to show their loyalty to her. To receive the morning star, then, is a symbolic expression of the statement which has gone before: the conqueror is doubly assured of participation with Christ in his sovereign activity within his Kingdom.

The fifth promise again is complex: the conqueror will be robed in white – having a holiness which contrasts with the soiled garments of the church in Sardis; his name will never be struck off the roll of the living, i.e. the register of the citizens of the Kingdom of God – a further apocalyptic representation of justification; and he will be confessed by Christ before the Father and his angels – an echo of words of Jesus in the synoptic Gospels (Matt. 10.32). The language conveys the conviction that election and redemption are in Christ and through Christ, and that the believer is dependent on him from first to last.

The sixth promise relates most closely of all to life in the city of God: 'I will make him a pillar in the temple of my God; he shall never leave it. And I will write the name of my God upon him, and the name of the city of my God, that new Jerusalem which is coming down out of heaven from my God, and my own new name' (3.12ff.). A more emphatic assurance of personal participation in the eternal city could not be imagined. The saying of a Jewish rabbi is called to mind: 'Three are named after the name of God, and these are the righteous, and the Messiah, and Jerusalem'; i.e. the righteous, the Messiah and Jerusalem belong to God. So the Christ declares that his faithful one belongs to the city of God, to God, and to himself at his glorious parousia.

The last promise is the crown of all: to the conqueror Christ grants to sit with him on his throne, as the Father granted him to sit with him on his throne (3.21). It is an emphatic assurance of sharing in the rule of Christ, alike in the millennial age and in the eternal Kingdom of the new creation. But the terms are breathtaking: as the Redeemer's conquest of the world in his obedience to death was rewarded with exaltation to the Father's side (cf. Phil. 2.9ff.), so the Christ honours him who maintains faith in him by fellowship with him in his eternal rule. And this is promised to the members of the church of Laodicea! Limitless forgiveness from infinite love reaches its apex here, and reassures us all who know our weakness.

Before we leave our consideration of John's vision of the city of God I would raise a question which is neglected by both writers on Christian eschatology and commentators on the Revelation: What effect, if any, does John's doctrine of the millennium have on his concept of eternal life? For the purpose of this lecture I assume that John does, in fact, present such a doctrine; the Augustinian equation of the millennium with the church age appears to be no longer tenable. Many however view this concept as an alien Jewish importation into the Christian understanding of the Kingdom of God. They maintain that in any case it is limited to a few verses in the 20th chapter of Revelation, and there it is limited to the rule of Christ with the martyrs. This opinion appears to me as mistaken as the Augustinian. The whole book of Revelation resounds with assurances to believers that they will participate in Christ's Kingdom: it is the burden of the promises to the conquerors and of the new song, to 'serve our God as priests, and they shall reign on earth' (5.9f.). So also at the conclusion of the messianic judgements a vast multitude exults for joy, because the wedding day of the Lamb has come, and his bride has made herself ready (19.6ff.); the Bride therefore appears with the Lamb, and so the city of God is revealed among men. That is, *the city descends to earth at the beginning and not at the end of Christ's earthly rule.* Consonant with this the brief description of the millennium in 20.4 ff. distinctly states that 'the camp of God's people and the city which he loves' is among men in that age, and that it is outrageously attacked. It is not unreasonable to conclude from this that John's description of the city of God in 21.9ff. relates first to the appearance of the city in history, in the reign of Christ among men. On this basis Revelation 19.11–21.5 gives a condensed narrative of events set in motion by the coming of the Lord to the end of time, and Revelation 21.9–22.5 contains a description of the city of God both in the earthly manifestation of Christ's rule and in the new creation. This is of course no novel interpretation; it was held by Theodor Zahn and by R. H. Charles, who however combined with it a complicated theory of editorial recension of the final chapters of Revelation.

When first I contemplated this possibility of interpreting the Revelation I was tempted to heave a sigh and recall the words of the song in the Mikado, 'Here's a How d'ye do!' What are we to make of this teaching? Light dawned for me with the simple recollection that John did not view the millennium as the initiation of the rule of Christ; he saw the Redeemer enthroned in his Easter event, and the rest of his sovereign acts as one with that. In this understanding he was not alone. Every line of the New Testament is written in the consciousness that the Kingdom of Christ is among men in the world now. John declared that Christ's coming will bring that Kingdom which is among men in this world *now* to decisive expression among men in this world *then*. The Kingdom initiated at Easter, manifested at the parousia and consummated in the new creation is one, reflecting one unbroken sovereign activity of the Christ. That has a corollary that the city of God is the dwelling of the redeemed now, that it will be manifested with Christ at his coming, and be the final dwelling of God and the new humanity in the eternal order. George Caird has worked out a thesis very similar to this in his exposition of Revelation; he maintains that it is of the nature of the city of God to descend from heaven to earth, so that the descent is not a single far-off divine event but a permanent spiritual fact; in a similar way the *glory* which dwells in the city has been anticipated in the experience of God's people, above all in the Incarnation, even as the *presence* of God in the city was with the Israelites in the desert, and supremely in Immanuel. If the description of the city in Revelation 21.9–27 be read in this light it will be seen that there is not a line of it which is not capable of realization in history – particularly as it is the Christ who brings it among men! But its perfected expression requires a transcendent order beyond earth's ability to give.

The lesson I draw from this is that the city to which we move is no strange place; we belong to it now, its powers are operative in the world now, and wherever they are known they transform. The grace which is to perfect the individual and society of which he is part has begun its work, and will bring it to completion. The second lesson is that the prayer which Jesus taught us will receive its answer in a more radical and yet more homely manner than the Church has commonly allowed; for God's Kingdom is to come and God's will shall be done among men on earth as it is in heaven. The scene of the hidden glory of the Incarnation is to be the scene of its manifest glory. The third lesson is more startling: if the city of God is to make heaven and earth one, man's awareness of heaven on earth will be far greater than he has known hitherto. How this is to be realized in the concrete relations of human existence John has not said, but his pictures suggest that the traffic between heaven and Charing Cross is going to increase mightily. Should this offend us? But why? Do we feel resentment that God may give to others what he has withheld from us? A parable of Jesus deals with a related problem to that, for in any case we shall be there. But as well might Moses complain that he was born before the Christ came. The prospect that the communion of the saints may be experienced as well as believed in, to the enrichment of all human life, should excite wonder and gratitude. The mode of its realization is as incomprehensible as the mode of life in heaven itself, but it is good to contemplate that one day heaven will not seem so remote to men as it does to most of us now.

Two issues call for consideration before we close our review. First, what light does Revelation shed on the state of the departed before the appearing of the city of God from heaven? Secondly, what does the book teach about judgement?

John's writing illustrates the attitude of the New Testament writers generally, whose eyes are so fixed on the manifestation of the Kingdom in the coming of Christ that the short time before the end is of little consequence. John devotes small space to this subject, but he says enough to reveal a lively view of the departed. The breaking of the fifth seal (6.19ff.) shows the martyrs beneath the altar, and they cry for vindication of their death. Why are they beneath the altar? The imagery has in view the fact that they have been sacrificed for God. Moreover in Jewish thought the altar is in the presence of God. 'He who is buried in the land of Israel is as if he were buried beneath the altar,' said Akiba, 'and he who is buried beneath the altar is as if he were buried beneath the throne of glory.' A later rabbi (Eliezer) affirmed, 'The souls of the righteous are hidden under the throne of glory.' What John said of the martyrs he would probably have extended to other Christian dead. But the martyrs have cause to be singled out: 'How long before you will judge and avenge our blood?' they ask, i.e. before God will vindicate their death by the reversal of the world's judgement in the revelation of the Kingdom. The righteous dead therefore pray! And their prayer is effective, for in chapter 8 it is answered by the signs of the end and the advent of the Kingdom of God (8.1–5). In Revelation therefore we have the phenomenon not of the living praying for the dead, but of the dead praying powerfully for the living.

The well known saying of 14.13, deserves notice: 'Happy are the dead who die in the faith of Christ!' We should then read on, not 'Henceforth', but '*Assuredly*, says the Spirit, they may rest from their labours, for they take with them the record of their deeds'. This is one of the seven beatitudes of the Revelation, and it is as seriously meant as the rest: '*Happy* are the dead!' The Holy Spirit emphasizes it: '*Assuredly* they are happy!' – so surely as they who are invited to the marriage supper of the Lamb are happy, privileged with grace and joy from God.

Lastly we recall that the Revelation gives many pictures of the redeemed in heaven joining in the worship offered by heaven. Most of these representations relate to the situation when God has answered his people's prayer for vindication, but in 19.1ff. we are shown a scene of exultation in heaven after the overthrow of the antigod power on earth; first the angelic orders offer praise to God, and then the vast crowd of the redeemed in heaven add their Alleluias, 'for the wedding day of the Lamb has come' (19.6f.). They joy in prospect of the event; it has not yet happened.

All this indicates that the happiness of those who *rest* from their labours is not of souls enjoying sound sleep, but the peace of those who know that their cause and their destiny are in the hands of God.

As to judgement, we all know that this features in the Revelation at length and in severity. There are two reasons for this. John has in view a situation in which men range themselves under the banner of a satanic Antichrist to obliterate the name and the cause of Christ from the earth; John's immediate cause of writing is to show how God will deal with the forces of evil which are bent on destroying God's world. The second motive is the pastoral purpose of warning all who profess faith in Christ not to yield to the pressures coming upon them and so lose their inheritance.

In this portrayal of the judgements John employs traditional images, above all those connected with the typology of the second exodus – hence his elaboration of the plagues of Egypt which fall on the kingdom of the new Pharoah. The example of the overthrow of the wicked in the destruction of Sodom also figures in his vision. These images John utilizes and adapts with complete freedom, often with a highly impressionist effect, which cannot be taken at all literally, and sometimes they are used inconsistently. An example of the latter is his descriptions of the overthrow of the anti-christian city: the doom song of chapter 18 utilizes Old Testament prophecies that tell of Babylon becoming a desolate silent ruin, haunted by wild beasts and demons of the desert; but the immediately succeeding song of heaven refers to the city's fate as akin to that of Sodom: 'Alleluia. The smoke goes up from her for ever!' New Babylon is to become a Sodom where destructive fires are never to go out. The two representations are inconsistent, but their use of the Scripture precedents for judgement is comprehensible. Observe, Babylon's fires last 'for ever'; but certainly not in the transcendent order of the new creation, when the works of the old order are abolished. John's pictures of judgement clearly require to be interpreted in the light of his general use of symbols and of his total doctrine. Some interpreters of the Revelation have been so impressed with John's more lurid delineations of judgement, they have assumed that he looked for the destruction of all mankind outside the Church. Since this often goes with the view that John anticipated the martyrdom of the whole Church, he must have wiped his slate very clean – nobody is left at the finish! John however was not an apocalyptic ecologist. He cherished hope for the world! If instead of letting the eye be captured by a few details in his picture we stand back and survey his whole canvas we discover that his hope for mankind was a great one and full of optimism: he looked for the world to be the scene of Christ's Kingdom, when the nations walk in the light of God's city and freely move in and out of its gates. He must have anticipated that the majority of earth's inhabitants would survive the rigours of the messianic judgements and so experience the blessings of the messianic reign. Such a man would not have expected the names in the book of life at the last judgement to be few. He certainly expected some to be omitted.

Many theories have been proposed concerning John's view of the ultimate destiny of evil men, and it is perhaps surprising how plausible are the arguments for his alleged universalism. With these I cannot deal. Of one thing we must be clear: John takes with deadly earnestness the reality of divine judgement, alike in history and beyond history; so do the rest of the New Testament writers who have left on record their thoughts about it, and I believe that we, too, should do likewise. John also recognized that the issues of eternity, as of history, are in God's hands. We surely should do the same, with faith and thankfulness.

The last words of the Revelation are a promise – 'I am coming soon'; then an assent thereto – 'Amen!'; and a prayer – 'Come, Lord Jesus!'; finally a benediction, 'The grace of the Lord Jesus be with you all'. We do well to give heed to the promise, add our own assent to it, pray our own prayer for it, and believe with unshakeable confidence that the grace of the enthroned Redeemer will be with us in life and in death, in this age and in the measureless ages of his invincible Kingdom.

God's Judgement of
the Individual after
Death

H. CUNLIFFE-JONES

A theologian who expounds the positive content of any
aspect of Christian eschatology in 1966 must take account
of the fact that he speaks into a generally indifferent or hostile
atmosphere, and out of a hesitant Christian tradition. This
means that he must first state his assumptions and procedure
before expounding the detailed content of Christian doctrine.

The justification of these assumptions is itself an urgent
and large subject. Christians must continually be ready to
give reasons why they hold the assumptions they do. But they
must also be prepared to explore the implications of the realities they trust in, and not let their spiritual vitality be sapped
by their sensitiveness to the prevalent scepticism. The
exploration of Christian resources is as necessary as the
attempt to show that the foundations of Christian faith are
true.

So, on the basis of certain assumptions, I shall speak to
Christian believers who share those assumptions, and to unbelievers who are prepared to hear how Christians develop
the implications of the assumptions they hold.

Criticism, which, in fact, implicitly contains a denial of one
or other of the assumptions will be out of place; though it
will be fair to ask whether these are assumptions Christians
ought to make, as well as to call attention to the points where
the insight or the argument limps.

125

1. THE ATMOSPHERE IN WHICH THE LECTURE IS
GIVEN

Let me first briefly elaborate on what I have said about the atmosphere in which the lecture is given. There is in it scepticism and indifference arising from a denial of any trans-empirical reality, and hesitancy and uncertainty in contemporary Christian eschatological affirmation.

(*a*) The scepticism and indifference spring at times from a widespread denial of anything that transcends the universe in which we live. Intramundane transcendence, for example, in the fact that a man's mind transcends his body and can roam through time and space, presents no problem or challenge. It is still an empirical phenomenon. It is the extra-mundane transcendence, essential to Christian faith, that is denied. Here, the Being of God, though active in the universe, is other than it and the living intelligent beings it contains. His being is beyond. To use the word 'beyond' is to use a metaphor, but it is an inescapable metaphor.

For the Christian, God transcends the universe in two ways at least: in being an Energy that is the source and controller of the energy that is within the universe; and in being a Goodness that is different in quality from the limited goodness found in human beings, and is the source from which human beings are transformed. Christians believe that there are experiences, which come from living within the universe, which point to the transcendent reality of God.

An illuminating contemporary illustration of the scepticism of our times is to be found in John Osborne's *Luther*. In this play Mr Osborne has gone to very great trouble indeed to get the historical details right, as indeed he has done. The one thing which vitiates his play is that he cannot himself believe that Luther honestly believed in God. He has set himself to present dramatically a man whose central experience, taken as true, is to the dramatist essentially meaningless. So he has tried to present Luther with a central meaning that

126

makes sense to the twentieth century – one in Osborne's view
that leaves out God as an actual reality.

It is against the background of such scepticism, and the
resulting indifference, that Christian theologians have to
expound the content of Christian truth.

(*b*) Christian eschatological teaching has not always followed one pattern, but for many centuries there has been
a standard and perfectly definite teaching. In this, the justice
of God finds complete satisfaction in the punishment of guilty
sinners in hell. God's order, shattered by sin, is entirely
restored by punishment. In addition, God, out of his super-
abundant mercy, has justified some and brought them to
eternal felicity with him. This is a further source of praise
to God, added to a divine ordering which in itself deserves
the highest praise, and is beyond all possible criticism.

But that that scheme is entirely consonant with the God
and Father of our Lord Jesus Christ has never won entire
assent, and for the last four centuries has been widely
questioned.[1] This questioning has set aside many things
repugnant now to the Christian mind and conscience, and
has brought about the possibility of a much more satisfying
Christian eschatology. But it has, for the time being, resulted
in a hesitance of affirmation which in itself is bad and a hurt
to the commendation of the Christian faith.

The hurt comes from uncertainty at the points where
confident and definite convictions are necessary to nourish
Christians with resources that are available in the Gospel.
This plea that current affirmations are less confident than
they ought to be is perfectly compatible with a sensitiveness
to the fact that our knowledge of the purpose of God and
of his Kingdom beyond death is less than our predecessors
thought it was. It is also compatible with serious criticism
of the traditional eschatology. We still need a positive
affirmation in a way that represents living conviction of
crucial Christian eschatological truths.

A concrete example of the hesitancy that has been upon

us may be seen in the hymns of English Congregationalism. If we compare the *Congregational Church Hymnal* of 1877 with the *Congregational Hymnary* of 1916 and this in turn with *Congregational Praise* published in 1951, we see a steady decline in confident affirmation. In 1877 there was at least one hymn, 'Great God, what do I see and hear', in which Christians were prepared to meet the judgement of God. The omission of the note of judgement has resulted in hurtful vagueness and sentimentality about the whole section.

Nor are Congregationalists alone in this hesitancy. If we look at the Service for the Burial of the Dead in the Alternative Services (Second Series), recommended by the Archbishops of Canterbury and York,[2] how faint is the note of judgement in it. It is true that one of the aims of the Burial Service is said to be 'to remind us of the awful certainty of our coming death and judgement'. But the adjective 'awful' is attached to certainty, and judgement seems to have been added perfunctorily. There is certainly no elucidation of what judgement means either in the Introduction or in the actual service.

2. FUNDAMENTAL ASSUMPTIONS

The Christian assumptions on which this lecture is based are first – the God of Christian faith incarnate in Christ; secondly, as corollaries of that: life after death and God's judgement on all men.

In the first assumption are two strands – God and God Incarnate. It may be that there are many who come to God only through Christ, but this is not universal, and historically, belief in God precedes belief in God incarnate. Belief in God is not co-terminous with Christian belief, however much for a Christian, his belief in God is saturated in what comes to him through his Christian allegiance. Yet if, for many, the way they came to any apprehension of God at all, or to any living faith in God, is through Christ and through Christ alone, they should be confident that this is a good way, provided that they really come to God. And if others come to Christ from apprehension of God, let them see to it that their understanding of God is thoroughly transformed by their discipleship to Christ.

To affirm God, let me make my own words used by Professor H. D. Lewis in his book, *Our Experience of God*. 'The object of religious experience is God, and whatever else we may find it possible to say about God, it is certain...that we must think of God as some reality complete and perfect in a way which is not possible for any other being or finite creature. He is the Creator, himself uncreated, the Lord God before whom we bow in worship which it would be blasphemous to render to any other, blasphemous and a violation of our own nature. The sole object of a genuine worship is a transcendent God.'[3]

The transcendent God is transcendent both in power and goodness. In calling him God we affirm that he is in control of the universe; we affirm also that he has a goodness which dwarfs ours.

Professor Lewis's definition is not explicitly Christian – but it is compatible with the Christian belief in one God, Father, Son and Holy Spirit, which has come from reflection on the fact of God incarnate in Jesus Christ.

Both elements of God's transcendence are to be found in the Incarnation – the ultimate power of God over nature in the Resurrection, and the ultimate goodness of God in the steadfast obedience of Jesus to his vocation, in love and forgiveness to the point of death. Both are necessary to the vitality of Christian faith.

It may be mentioned here that the notes which Dietrich Bonhoeffer jotted down as part of an outline for a book have exercised a misleading fascination for many minds. He certainly would not have kept strictly to them in the writing of the actual book.

He wrote: 'What do we mean by "God"? Not in the first

place an abstract belief in his omnipotence, etc. This is not a genuine experience of God, but a partial extension of the world. Encounter with Jesus Christ, implying a complete orientation of human being in the experience of Jesus as one whose only concern is for others. This concern of Jesus for others the experience of transcendence. This freedom from self, maintained to the point of death, the sole ground of his omnipotence, omniscience and ubiquity. Faith is the participation in this Being of Jesus (incarnation, cross and resurrection). Our relation to God is not religious relationship to a supreme Being, absolute in power and goodness, which is a spurious conception of transcendence, but a new life for others through participation in the Being of God. The transcendence consists not in tasks beyond our scope and power, but in the nearest thing to hand. God in human form, not, as in other religions . . . but man existing for others, and hence the Crucified. A life based on the transcendent.'[4]

Positively, this is a passionate affirmation for recognition that in the utter selflessness of Jesus there is a quality of goodness which constrains our worship and demands our transformation.

Negatively, it is a repudiation of other aspects of Lutheran theology which, however, he still continues to presuppose, as in his reference to the omnipotence, omniscience and ubiquity of Jesus. As a plea for recognition of a special emphasis, it is moving and convincing: as a total theology it is absurd. What Bonhoeffer was most deeply concerned to affirm finds its true place in the Christian belief in God both as Creator and Redeemer: and this is the belief which is presupposed in this lecture.

In addition to this fundamental assumption, the lecture presupposes *two corollaries from it* – the first *life after death*, the second *God's judgement on all men*.

Christian belief in *life after death* is based on a conviction that Jesus Christ in his life, death and resurrection won a victory over sin and death.

Belief in life after death has at times been widespread in human life, but it comes to Christian faith in three ways: through the faith which came to life in Judaism through the suffering and death of the Maccabean martyrs; through the teaching of Jesus; and through the resurrection of Jesus himself.

The ground for believing in life after death is not human wishes but the purpose of God. God is sovereign over the universe, and will bring purpose to fulfilment. Human life after death has its place within the fulfilment of God's purpose for the universe. He has created human beings for fellowship with himself and he cannot allow this to be frustrated by death. This affirmation goes back a long way in Christian theology: it is developed in the thinking of the early centuries.

The second corollary to the fundamental assumption of one God incarnate in Christ is *God's judgement on all men*.

Life after death in fulfilment of God's purpose means life on God's terms. Whatever the view taken of the meaning of God's judgement, life on God's terms means that human life must submit to it. And this applies to all men. We know that God's purpose is not for a section only, but for the whole of mankind. In the New Testament we read (1 Tim. 2.3–4) of 'God our Saviour. He wants everyone to be saved and reach full knowledge of the truth.' If his purpose is to be fulfilled, then all men must come to the point of being judged by God's standard, and beyond that share in the fellowship of his everlasting Kingdom. The problems connected with the possibility or impossibility of this are many and their solution is not part of the initial assumptions of this lecture. What is being assumed is that judgement is a necessary corollary of believing in God. None of us can escape the·judgement of the everlasting God.

3. THE PRECISE NATURE OF THE SUBJECT WITHIN THE ASSUMPTIONS

Let us make clear the precise nature of the subject within the assumptions I have laid down. I do not deny that God's judgement is experienced on earth, but I do not believe that it is wholly experienced here. The transition of anyone beyond death raises important questions for Christian thinking about the worth of life and any commitment we make within it, and so I have chosen to speak on God's judgement of the individual after death. I do not speak of judgement at the Lord's Coming, because I believe that that term should now be used just as a symbol for the final Kingdom of God. Within that final Kingdom there are two distinguishable but related aspects – of which the more difficult to formulate is God's judgement on the corporate life of man in history and his final triumph. The other aspect is God's judgement of the individual for which we ought to prepare ourselves. It is about this second aspect that I have chosen to speak. Let me say that in doing so I have not attempted to formulate a theory either of the relation between time an¹ eternity or of the relation between corporate and individu judgement.

4. THE NATURE OF GOD'S JUDGEMENT

What is the nature of God's judgement?

God's judgement is the bringing of man inescapably before the standard that God gives him, so that in repentance and adoration he may respond, if he will, to the transforming grace of God. This standard is given in Christ in whom there is both sternness and compassion. God's judgement is all the more searching and intimate because it is the judgement of the Incarnate Lord. And this is so whether we come from Christ to God, or from God to Christ. The element of punishment is to be found in the restraint of the wicked and the self-exclusion from the presence of God of those who finally refuse to respond to his judgement. But in God's purpose, judgement is an instrument of mercy and a means of transforming the sinner.

This theme may be expounded under four heads:

1. *God's Standard*

The character of God is the crucial fact in the universe and to find their true being all things must conform to him, and his standard for them must become actual in them. Judgement means being inescapably confronted with God's standard for ourselves.

Human life is a strange compound of freedom and possible fulfilment. By *freedom* I mean the negative freedom to dissent. By *fulfilment* I mean the realization of the true possibilities in anyone's life. Many theologians use the term 'freedom' to cover both meanings, but this is the source of confusion and untruth. God asks man for a response in freedom, but his nature is such that he has no true fulfilment except in conformity to God's standard. Uncertainty still hangs over the reaching of this fulfilment.[5]

Judgement means being confronted by God so that his standard is made clear before us. In itself it is our total satisfaction. Yet because of the perversity ingrained in us, it and God who requires it, are to some extent hateful to us. That element of hatefulness has to be overcome before we can attain the satisfaction of our lives. This is the element of judgement which produces dread. But God's standard is the fact that our lives have a positive meaning and that we can share in the purpose God gives to the universe.

2. *In Christ*

In the New Testament and in the life of the Church, judgement is ascribed to Christ. We may note the word of the Fourth Gospel: 'The Father judges no one; he has entrusted all judgement to the Son, so that all may honour the Son as they honour the Father' (John 5:22, 23). We may note also the fact that in the Apostles' Creed it is of 'Jesus Christ his only Son our Lord' of whom it is said 'from thence he shall come to judge the quick and the dead'.

From the portrait of Jesus in the Gospels in all the ebb and flow of the wrestle for historical reliability, two traits stand out: his sternness and his compassion. The Jewish leaders did not resolve to ensure his death out of unmotivated malice: they sought to remove one who was a menace to all they stood for. It was not only a wonderful experience for the disciples to be with Jesus: it was clearly also an uncomfortable one. At any moment, through their blundering misunderstanding of the nature of his mission, they would say some word or take some action that would bring on them his sharp rebuke. They trusted him and longed to be with him: but they were afraid of him, too. The crowd which welcomed him in many ways, had come to realize some of his unwavering insistence on putting God first before they shouted for his death.

The evidence for his generous compassion, his giving new heart and hope to many who had lost it, is too great to be ignored. But all he did in the healing of body and soul was not at any point a capitulation to immediate need, or to temporary success; it was always kept firmly in the direction of his mission. His demand for the utter obedience of heart and mind is all a piece with his seeking and saving the lost.

So the judgement of the incarnate Lord is all the more searching and intimate because it is the judgement of the incarnate Lord.

This is so whether we come from Christ to God or from God to Christ.

In the sceptical atmosphere of contemporary experience, I want to affirm, though it may be offensive to many who will cheerfully say that *God* is dead, that the importance of *Christ* is *logically* just as questionable as the reality of God.

H. Cunliffe-Jones

If we discount the historical importance of the Christian
Church with its conviction that Jesus is the light of the world
at its centre; if we then ask why we should consider important
for the experience of the twentieth century one who, on a
neutral basis, is a first-century prophet who died an enthu-
siast's death, the answer is not very clear unless we assume
that the Christian faith in him is true. But many who are
confused and uncertain about *God*, find *Christ* in some way
given to them. This comes, whether they know it or not, from
the continuing influence of the Christian tradition.

But whether logically justified or not, many do find a way
from Christ to God.[6] They find a challenge in his words and
actions and in the whole intent of his life. They feel impelled
to find an explanation of them all that satisfies their minds.
At the heart of Jesus they find an utter goodness that impels
them to think of it as not having its source in this intra-mun-
dane sphere. The holiness of Jesus is their route for knowing
God in his transcendence. And this can be a genuine awareness of one aspect of transcendent God.

For all such people who come from Christ to God, the
judgement of God, just because it is the judgement of the
incarnate Lord, is inevitably intimate and searching.

But this is also true for others who come the other way
from God to Christ. We have learnt through Karl Barth not
to set over against Christ a God of majestic but inscrutable
power to whom we can give terror but not true worship.
There is majesty in God, but it is a majesty in which God's
power is the instrument of his wisdom and his love. And he
has expressed that wisdom and love in Christ. Men have
often rebelled against God interpreted as an alien tyrant,
whose judgement, though inescapable, was in essence unfair
and unrelated to a true understanding of those whom he
judged. But God in Christ understands our life from within.
His judgement is not alien but intimate.

His is the searching judgement which is utterly true and
reveals ourselves to ourselves, and lights up aspects of

135

ourselves which we do not expose to our own scrutiny, so that against it we are defenceless. The judgement of God in Christ is one that we ourselves, when we come to know it, must acknowledge as a true and perfect judgement.

3. *The Element of Punishment*

Punishment is an idea which is little stressed in the New Testament, though the emphasis on punishment has had a large place in the history of Christian eschatology. Certain passages in the New Testament have exercised a hold on Christian imagination until the seventeenth century out of all proportion to their importance in the New Testament itself.

We may mention particularly Matt. 25.46: 'they will go away to eternal punishment, and the virtuous to eternal life'; 2 Thess. 1.7–11 especially v. 9: 'It will be their punishment to be lost eternally, excluded from the presence of the Lord and from the glory of his strength'; 2 Peter 2.9: 'hold the wicked for their punishment until the day of Judgement'; Rev. 14.9–11: 'All those who worship the beast and his statue, or have had themselves branded on the hand or forehead, will be made to drink the wine of God's fury which is ready, undiluted, in his cup of anger; in fire and brimstone they will be tortured in the presence of the holy angels and the Lamb and the smoke of their torture will go up for ever and ever.' (*Jerusalem Bible*)

Punishment, however, ought not to have the same place in a present-day statement of Christian eschatology. And we have learnt to revise our notions of punishment. The Jesuit teacher, Fr Joseph Rickaby, wrote in 1929, 'The punishment for final persistent defiance of the natural law is failure to attain to the perfect state and last end of the human soul, which is happiness. If existence is prolonged, under this failure, it must be in the contrary state of misery. This failure and misery is at once a natural result and Divine affliction.'[7]

This is in many ways a most attenuated idea of punish-

ment, and it is only such an attenuated doctrine that rightly
has its place in our understanding of God's judgement.

The element of punishment in a true doctrine of God's
judgement consists first of being confronted by the standard
of God of which we have already spoken. In the very fact
of this, we are rebuked for our falling short of it, and for our
active hostility to it. Other elements are the restraint of the
wicked; and the self-exclusion from the presence of the Lord
of those who finally refuse to respond to his judgement. In
all these ways the authority of God is newly asserted in relation to the sinner. The second and third aspects have still
to be considered.

(a) *Restraint of the Wicked*

About the restraint of the wicked we may say this. Human
life is lived under the burden of the temporal power of wicked
men, and with evil in nature and in human life a distressing
enigma. The greatness of the Psalms is to be seen in the fact
that they acknowledge this fully, and yet affirm a strong, confident faith in God.

> Yahweh, how much longer are the wicked,
> how much longer are the wicked to triumph?
> Are these evil men to remain unsilenced,
> boasting and asserting themselves?
> Yahweh, they crush your people,
> they oppress your hereditary people,
> murdering and massacring
> widows, orphans and guests.
>
> 'Yahweh sees nothing,' they say
> 'the God of Jacob takes no notice.'
>
> (Psalm 94.3–7)
>
> Why does the wicked man spurn God,
> assuring himself, 'He will not make me pay'?
>
> (Psalm 10.13)

The judgement of God inevitably means that the power of the wicked to oppress others is taken away. God will for ever respect the freedom of man, and will not compel a positive response to his outpoured grace. But the wickedness of man will be restrained so that it does not oppress others as it does here in our earthly life. What form this restraint will take is beyond our knowledge.

(b) *Self-exclusion from the Presence of the Lord*

For centuries Christians believed that the perpetual exclusion of countless sinners from the presence of the Lord was a necessary part of Christian faith. There has been a widespread movement away from this even to the extent of the insensitiveness to the stern element in the Gospel. It must, however, be realized that if men come into God's eternal Kingdom, it can only be on God's terms. Anyone who contemplates the sinfulness of the life of man must realize that its transformation into the holiness God seeks to give to man is a stupendously great work. We can be sure of the inevitability of each human life being confronted by God's judgement: we can be sure that it is God's will to save all men; and we can be sure that he will respect human freedom. We also know that if there is any self-exclusion from the presence of the Lord, this will be to that extent a failure of God's hopes and purposes. But the possibility of such self-exclusion seems to be a necessary element in the presentation of the Gospel, if we are not to minimize either the demand of God or the dignity of man.

It may be said that this is faint-hearted affirmation. Rather we ought to say that we *know* that in the end all will be saved. God is the infinite God, and there is no limit to his striving, and so to the accomplishment of his purposes. Limited, finite man cannot in the end do anything but conform to the purpose of God. However painful to the sinner the process of reclamation, we *know*, it may be said that in the end God's Kingdom will be complete.

But this thinking goes against the true and important thesis so powerfully argued in John Oman's *Grace and Personality*[8] – that we fundamentally distort the Gospel if we make God's relation to us that of an infinite force.

Just because of the urgent need of man to respond inwardly to the judgement of God in which lies the possibility of his true life, we must *keep open* the possibility that some, in the personal freedom that God will not crush, will exclude themselves from the presence of God.

4. *The Instrument of God's Mercy and his Means of Transforming the Sinner*

Many people seem to treat judgement and mercy as if they were opposed: as if mercy was a soft word applicable to a God of love, and judgement a hard word applicable to a God with a very different attribute. But God's love is deep and strong: it does not cease until it has attained the true well-being of its object. It is the love of our Incarnate God. How else shall he love us except by bringing us into his Kingdom? Truly to love us means to persist in judging and cleansing us so that we may wholly respond to his love.

This is why judgement, although it has an element of dread in it, is fundamentally a welcome and hopeful word. It is the gateway to God's mercy, or rather it is an instrument of his mercy. God has no other desire for us than that all men should be saved and come to the knowledge of the truth. It is his *mercy* that men really shrink from if they did but know it. For he has made it plain in the Cross of Christ that his love is not to be traded upon. And so the Bible testifies, in both Old Testament and New. The psalmist insists that it is a fool who says in his heart that there is no God (Psalm 14.1); and the apostle warns us that God is not to be cheated (Gal. 6.7), or, to express it more colloquially, you can't fool God. His mercy is relentless in his pursuance of the redemption of the sinner.

So God's judgement is to be seen as his means of trans-

formation. It is by confronting the sinner with the full implications of his call to be a child of God in fellowship with him,
and with the full horror of the sin that defiles that relationship, that God will bring the sinner, if he will respond, into
his Kingdom. Some of the glory of God in the face of Jesus
Christ which brings its inevitable judgement of the unworthy, we see in part here on earth, and to it we make a
partial and possibly a growing response. This is Christian
discipleship – to be laid hold of by God's judgement in Christ
Jesus and to be made new in conformity with his standard.
His final judgement is the completion of the work already
begun. However painful it is, the purpose of it is healing and
restorative.

Apart from God's judgement, how shall its purposes be
effective in us? Christ's identification of himself with the
judgement of God on sin has shown us the way to eternal
life. In Christ we can truly share in God's goodness as we
totally and completely identify ourselves with his judgement.
This is the means of transformation and the ground of hope.

This positive aspect of judgement is finely expressed in
Robert Murray McCheyne's hymn:[9]

> When I stand before the throne,
> Dressed in beauty not my own,
> When I see Thee as Thou art,
> Love Thee with unsinning heart,
> Then, Lord, shall I fully know,
> Not till then, how much I owe.

That is the goal of Christian life: but how we must be
judged and cleansed before that happens! And this longing
and expectation so far from excluding judgement on earth
helps to enable us to enter into it.
So the hymn ends:

> E'en on earth, as through a glass,
> Darkly let Thy glory pass;

140

Make forgiveness feel so sweet;
Make Thy Spirit's help so meet;
E'en on earth, Lord, make me know
Something of how much I owe.

5. GOD'S JUDGEMENT OF THE INDIVIDUAL AFTER DEATH

If this, then, is the nature of God's judgement of the individual after death, how shall we think of it?

It is a *great reality* the full meaning of which we can never exhaust, which is partly apprehended in our earthly life.

It is a *reality from which we shrink*, because of the holiness of the presence of God, and because we shall be unable to escape from full awareness of our own unworthiness. Yet it is also *the means through which we can enjoy God for ever* in the utter fulfilment of our lives.

So it is a source of *assurance, hope, and joy*.

God's judgement is mystery – that is, *a reality which is so great that we can never exhaust its meaning*. This does not mean something totally incomprehensible: every true mystery has a centre of light. As we accustom ourselves to its reality we understand it more, but even so we can never fully comprehend the reality which in varying degrees we apprehend. God's judgement is a mystery which is 'dark through brightness', and partially hidden by its very 'splendour of light', though God's greatness is also hidden by human sinfulness.

For God's judgement is not only a great reality: it is a reality from which we shrink. And yet it is a reality for which we deeply long: for it is the means through which we can enjoy God for ever.

Truly to come into the presence of God is to become aware of his holiness – that holiness incarnate in Christ. Holiness is utter goodness with a splendour about it that cannot be hid. In our human sin-conditioned world we live with blurred shades of goodness. Every country in every century needs outstanding examples of Christian holiness to provide near at hand a greater approximation to the true holiness of God. The nearer awareness of that holiness will be an experience so far-reaching that we shrink from being made to revise our fragmentary understanding of what utter goodness is, by the presence of the absolute goodness of God.

Here we experience the true object of worship: the one to whom man's worship with heart and mind and soul and strength is rightly given; the one in whom true fulfilment of man's being is found. But we have not given that kind of worship. We have spurned his proffered love. And so we shrink from it because it is too great for us.

One of the difficulties of our earthly life is to accept ourselves without illusions. Even when we have learnt to be self-critical, there is always a hidden part of ourselves that does not come up for our criticism. The element in God's judgement which we shrink from is that we will have to accept ourselves in the light of God's presence.

For, however far we have progressed in the Christian life, Christians presenting themselves in Christ Jesus for God's judgement, have still to be tested and transformed by the full knowledge of God and the full transformation of our lives. The nearer we have approached to Christian perfection in this life, the more we will acknowledge and welcome the searching experience that lies ahead. For that judgement will show us truly to ourselves as we are, and we will acknowledge it to be fair. This will not diminish the pain of it – the pain of fully exposing ourselves for God's cleansing. But this cleansing is the only way to the fulfilment and utter satisfaction of our whole being in the everlasting God.

John Calvin gave expression to a notable expression of thanksgiving for God's judgement when he said: 'Awakened consciences, when they have to do with God's judgement, recognize this as the only safe haven in which they can securely breathe.'[10] Earlier he had said: 'Hence arises a wonderful consolation: that we perceive judgement to be in the hands of him who has already destined us to share with him the honour of judging (cf. Matt. 19.28) . . . for if the Apostle dares exclaim that with Christ interceding for us there is no one who can come forth to condemn us (Rom. 8.33, 34), it is much more true, then, that Christ as Intercessor will not condemn those whom he has received into his charge and protection. No mean assurance this, that we shall be brought before no other judgement seat than that of our Redeemer, to whom we must look for our salvation! Moreover, he who now promises eternal blessedness through the Gospel, will then fulfil his promise in judgement.'[11]

The reasons for thinking that God's judgement gives us an atmosphere in which at last we can breathe freely are that we are delivered from atmospheres which poison our spiritual vitality; and if we respond to God's judgement we shall become most truly ourselves and most truly set free from all that thwarts and hinders our inner being. So we shall be set free to enjoy for ever God who is the centre and fulfilment of our lives.

God's judgement after death is certain. It is *assurance* that God is a living and active God. He will not allow his purpose to be frustrated, he will not let his children go to ruin, without doing his utmost to transform and deliver them. It is only the utterly recalcitrant who determinedly refuse to respond to his judgement who may possibly defeat his purpose.

It is *hope* that gives us encouragement in a sinful world in which we see his name taken in vain, his very existence scorned, his redemption in Christ ignored or repudiated, his standard for human living denied in the individual and corporate life of man. God's judgement is hope that this is not the total experience of human life. God will bring all human experience to the bar of his transforming judgement.

It is *joy* that the everlasting God really cares for mankind. Apart from his judgement there is no final assurance of his love. His coming in Christ has not done its full work. It is the completion of that work that will reveal its true greatness.

143

That that completion is certain is a source of joy that cannot be contained. God calls us to pass through his judgement to share in his serenity and blessedness. This faith is the source of our rejoicing. To God belong the Kingdom, the Power, and the Glory for ever.

NOTES

1. See, for example, D. P. Walker's researches into seventeenth-century discussions of eternal torment in his book, *The Decline of Hell*, (Routledge and Kegan Paul, 1964); James P. Martin, *The Last Judgement in Protestant Theology from Orthodoxy to Ritschl* (Oliver and Boyd, 1963); and Ulrich Simon, *The End is Not Yet* (Nisbet, 1964).
2. SPCK, 1965.
3. Allen and Unwin, 1959, p. 65.
4. *Letters and Papers from Prison*, Fontana, 1963, pp. 164–5.
5. cf. the discussion by Paul Tillich on freedom and destiny, *Systematic Theology*, vol. II, Nisbet, 1957, pp. 72–3.
6. cf. *A Religion for Agnostics* by Nathaniel Micklem, SCM, 1965.
7. *Moral Philosophy*, quoted by Lord Longford in *The Idea of Punishment*, Geoffrey Chapman, 1961, p. 93.
8. Cambridge University Press, first published 1917.
9. *Congregational Praise* 772.
10. *Institutes*, III. xii. 4.
11. ibid. II. xvi. 18.

The Hope of Glory

H. F. LOVELL COCKS

When the Drew lectureship was founded the destiny of the individual after death was virtually the only aspect of Christian eschatology to focus the attention of our preachers and thinkers. And even so, the attention was no more than perfunctory and fitful. For the main preoccupation of that generation was not with the destiny of the individual in the next world but with his prospects of deliverance from injustice and oppression in this. On the whole such teaching as was given on the theme of immortality seems to have been inadequate to the spiritual needs of bereaved and grief-stricken hearts. This is the inference one draws from the great vogue of spiritualism during and immediately after the first world war. The neglect of the subject was no doubt partially responsible for the overlooking of the wide difference between the philosophical conception of immortality and the Christian doctrine of the Resurrection. In so far as it was no longer possible to believe in the literal reconstitution of the material body, the New Testament imagery had to be taken as a symbolical representation of the truth more exactly expressed by the philosophical conception of the immortality of the soul. Admittedly it was a very awkward and misleading symbolism, but the only alternative to treating it thus was to take it in the most matter-of-fact literalness as teaching the resurrection of the flesh. And of course there have never been wanting extreme theological conservatives who have done this very thing in defiance of all comers. But in fact conservatives and their modernist opponents have been equally at fault here – as extremists so often are who fight about the Bible instead of pondering over what is

145

written there. Here, for example, neither side seems to have given any close study to the fifteenth chapter of the first Epistle to the Corinthians. A careful reading of that chapter would have convinced the conservatives that, so far from endorsing, the Apostle expressly repudiates an interpretation of immortality that implies the reconstitution of that fleshly body that moulders in the grave. The modernists for their part would have discovered that whatever Paul meant by resurrection he did not in the very least mean what Plato meant when he spoke of the immortality of the soul.

But not only was the New Testament conception of resurrection misconceived at this time, but the tremendous doctrines of a Last Judgement and a Final Consummation of all things were almost entirely given up. The dominant liberal Protestantism of the day had discarded belief in the Second Coming of Christ as belonging to the temporary Jewish husk of the Christian Gospel, and had put in its place an evolutionary conception of history with its cheerful prospect of a world growing every day and in every way better and better. To occupy the ground thus abandoned there moved in self-styled students of prophecy with their tortuous ingenuity and crass literalism. In our time the notion of a realized eschatology has done much to recover for us the authentic Christian outlook; yet there is more in the New Testament doctrine of the Last Things than can be brought within the framework of this new and valuable conception. The Last Judgement and Final Consummation of all things are not subsidiary and peripheral features of the New Testament witness. They are central to it, and the Christian Gospel of redemption is incomplete – I had almost said, impotent – where they are not seen to be the keystone of the whole. The logic of our Christian belief follows a simple pattern. We have no assurance of final salvation from sin and death unless he who saves us is Creator and Lord of all things. It was in the strength of this conviction that the Christian Church resisted Gnosticism in the second century and Arianism in the fourth.

And by the same logic we have no certitude of an everlasting
life of blessedness in the presence of God except in the final
and complete victory of the righteous God over every power
that might destroy us. So it comes about that our faith in
our personal immortality is grounded neither in the evidence
supplied by the Society for Psychical Research nor in the
time-honoured arguments which purport to establish the
simplicity and indestructibility of soul-substance, nor in anything less fundamental and all-embracing than the holy love
and almighty power of a divine Father revealed in his saving
deeds as Creator and Sovereign Ruler of the worlds.

Let us now remind ourselves what we believe concerning
God. We believe that the God and Father of our Lord Jesus
Christ is also the Father and Saviour of all who put their
trust in him. We believe that every one of his children is dear
to his heart and that like the good shepherd who seeks his
sheep until he finds it, our God follows us with his grace in
all the devious ways of our sinful wanderings until we turn
to him and are reconciled. We believe that this love of his
is so great and high that only the cross of his dear Son can
measure it or make manifest the price that the Father is ready
to pay for the redemption of the lowest and least of us. We
also believe that the love of the Father towards us is an everlasting love, and that he will neither weary of us nor suffer
us at our last hour for any pains of death to fall from him.
We believe in his gracious promise of eternal life. But we can
believe these things only because we believe that our Father
is also King of Kings and Lord of Lords, who is able to bring
to pass all that his holy love has decreed concerning us. We
dare to believe that we shall live again after death because
we believe that he is able to keep what we have entrusted
to him against that day. We believe not in the survival of
some indestructible immaterial part of us, but in the resurrection of the body, that is, the redemption of our entire personality. And our faith takes a still wider sweep. We believe
that our putting on of immortality is the signal for the renewal

of the whole creation, which waits for the manifestation of the sons of God.

There is a maxim of jurisprudence that demands not only that justice be done but that it shall be seen to be done. God's justice has been done once for all on the cross of Christ crucified and risen. There God's righteousness was revealed and secured for ever. There the decisive battle in God's campaign against sin and death was fought and won. But all this is known only to the man of faith. God's victory over evil is manifest only to those who can rejoice in the resurrection of Christ and worship their risen Lord. In the eyes of unbelievers the victory is no victory but disastrous and irretrievable defeat. Therefore the Christ who on earth lived as a carpenter and suffered as a criminal must return in glory. The Son of man who first came in obscurity must come again 'on the clouds of heaven'. It is not easy to demythologize the New Testament even where that operation is most obviously necessary. But at least we can see that this coming on the clouds of heaven represents the justification of God and his gracious purposes, the vindication of Christ and his cross on the great stage of the world and to the discomfiture and confusion of all gainsayers and enemies of his righteousness. For when he comes again, 'every eye shall see him'. We have to stretch our minds to conceive – we cannot hope to imagine – this 'Second Coming'. It is an event that is not an event – since it is history's consummation and not its continuation. It is a coming which is not a coming – since he who comes is already here in the plenitude of his power. Yet if it is hard for our thought to grasp the end of all things and the winding up of history, that fact ought not to surprise or disconcert us. The Last Things are not more intractable to our thought than the First Things, and finite minds that cannot easily conceive the end of the world are just as much at a loss to conceive its beginning. Creation is not a fact among the facts we can comprehend and classify. Here, too, we have an event that does not belong to that series of events we call history. For creation is the pre-condition of events, not as coming before them, but as determining and in a sense containing them. So, too, the end of the world is not the last happening in a series of happenings, but the inner meaning and ultimate significance of them all.

In truth there is more than analogy between creation and final redemption. These two belong together within the ambit of our Christian faith, so that to lose assurance of one is to lose it of the other too. In the second century the life of the Church was threatened by Gnosticism. Now Gnosticism was a way of thinking which, from the best of motives, attempted to drive a wedge between the Old Testament and the New, between creation and redemption, and between the Creator and the Saviour. The Gnostic objection to creation was that it was a work unworthy of the supreme God, who was too pure to soil his hands with the finite and the mutable, and from whose wisdom nothing so gross as this material world could issue forth. It was given to the Church to discern that what was threatened here was nothing less than the very heart of the Gospel. It was seen that we are not saved unless the Creator saves us; that there can be no final redemption, no complete triumph over evil, no eternal blessedness, unless he who redeems us and promises us life everlasting is none other than the almighty Maker and Lord of all things. But today the stress must also fall on the Final Judgement and the consummation of the New Creation. It is the same battle we fight – the battle for the right to believe that the all-powerful Creator and the all-loving Redeemer are one God world without end. The great circle of the creation is closed in the Last Judgement and the summing up of all things in Christ. We need not be ashamed because our thought cannot grasp what our faith must affirm. The Lord God Omnipotent reigneth.

Some people tell us that we ought not to hope for our personal immortality. They say that these little selves of ours with their queer oddities and angularities have no legitimate claim to immortality and the prospect of their enduring for ever should fill all right-thinking men and women with disgust. Of course it is natural that we should wish to go on living for ever. But that wish is stamped with a childish egoism that we should strive to outgrow. Can we seriously claim that we are worthy of immortality?

Now it is true that men have often desired immortality from selfish motives and have conceived the life beyond in puerile and unsatisfying ways. We may desire immortality like little boys who want the school holidays to last for ever. We may wish some state of real or imagined comfort prolonged in some lotus-land where it is always afternoon. Or on the other hand we may wish that some loved and delightful activity may be endlessly possible to us. Or we may simply desire 'the wages of going on, and not to die'. Yet not for these reasons have the saints longed for eternal life. In the Old Testament the doctrine of resurrection first makes its appearance as the answer to the prayers of the righteous remnant who knowing, like Job, that their Vindicator lived, desired to see the day of the Lord and to share in the victory of their God. And in all ages men who have walked with God and tasted his goodness have hoped for immortality not that they might please themselves without limit, but that they might glorify their Lord more fully, and do his will more perfectly, and enjoy for ever the blessedness of his nearer presence.

The desire for immortality, therefore, may be a truly sanctified desire. And it is surely plain that if immortality means anything, it means personal immortality, the immortality of your individual self and mine. To talk of values being conserved though persons are extinguished is to talk the veriest nonsense. When we speak of immortality we are concerned not with values in general nor with the eternal verities but with the value of the individual John Smith to the God who created him and who loves him with an everlasting love.

The Drew lecturer is commissioned to give his hearers

assurance regarding the reality of eternal life. That assurance has now been given. 'Let not your hearts be troubled, ye believe in God.' To believe with our whole hearts in the God and Father of our Lord Jesus Christ is to be delivered from the fear of death and to be given assurance of everlasting life. We are loved with a love that will not let us go.

So here we might stop, were it not for the questions that perennially rise in the minds of believers. Now our questionings need not betoken fundamental doubt. It is well to remember this, for there is much that will remain unknown to us this side of the veil, and our faith must learn to wait in a serene and patient agnosticism for the breaking of the seals and the opening of the book. Some questions, however, can be partially answered. Eternal life for you and me involves the redemption and perfecting of our finitude, and most of the questions that are so insistent centre round the nature of this redemption. What difference will it make to us when this corruptible puts on incorruption and this mortal immortality?

'He that believeth hath eternal life.' We get a foretaste of heaven here. And we may look to the characteristic glories of our life in the Spirit to give us some far-off glimpse of the glory that shall be ours hereafter. But first we must try to understand the meaning of our finitude, for our immortality is not its negation but its fulfilment. Our human personalities are not destined to annihilation nor to absorption into the Infinite. The Christian religion diverges sharply from every mysticism of the pantheistic type. John Smith will retain his individuality, even in heaven. His finitude is destined to be redeemed, not extinguished. Though he was not created to be immortal in his own right, Smith is destined for immortality. True, Smith is nothing in himself – yet he is not nothing. For God has made him something.

> Thou wilt not leave us in the dust;
> Thou madest man, he knows not why –

151

He thinks he was not made to die:
And Thou hast made him: Thou art just.

And it is because God has made him – the God revealed in Christ – that man may know that he was not made to die but to live for ever in blessed communion with his heavenly Father. For God has made man a responsible creature. Responsibility is the very hall-mark of selfhood. To be a man is to be a creature capable of making a response – a free, intelligent response – to God. There is nothing in our Gospel to suggest that God made us responsible beings only to use us as raw material for some higher type of creature. Higher creatures than man there may be – and they also are the objects of God's love and care. But it was not for the holy angels but for sinful men that Christ died, and the whole tenor of the Gospel makes it certain that our eternal destiny according to the loving purpose of God is not to be merged in the infinity of his being like raindrops in the ocean, but to stand a hand's breadth off that he may continue to be gracious to us and we may continue to give him our love and obedience in an everlasting communion.

But flesh and blood cannot inherit the Kingdom of God. What then are the marks of our finitude, and in what way can we suppose them modified when this mortal shall have put on immortality?

In the first place, a finite personality is subject to desire. Our lives are made up of wants and longings and of the thoughts and acts whereby we attempt to satisfy them. As with the animals so with us desire stems from vital need and is a spur to action. Like the animals we suffer pain when circumstances obstruct or frustrate our striving. Yet unlike the animals we seem to be able to bring our desires into clear consciousness and deliberate whether we shall gratify one rather than another which competes with it, or whether we shall prefer a greater to a lesser good and a long-term satisfaction to the pleasure of the moment. Now what spoils us as finite personalities is what we call sin – which is the corruption of our finitude just as eternal life is its perfection and crown. According to our Christian Gospel man's supreme good is God himself and man's chief end to glorify God and enjoy him for ever. That is to say, man was created to desire God above all other goods. To the attainment of this supreme good, all lesser goods, even life itself, must be subjected. This is not to deny the place and value of these lesser goods. But their place is never the first place, and their value is always instrumental. They are means to an end; stepping stones towards the soul's true goal – communion with God. When we forget this we turn our backs on God, our chief good, and organize our lives round some lesser good. The desire for this good then begins to dominate the rest. It becomes our ruling passion and lust is born. And because only God can be the true centre of our lives, this new organization of our desires is but disorganization, anarchy and chaos. What is more, the usurping desire itself becomes disordered and seeks unnatural satisfactions; it becomes a hunger that craves not bread but stones. The New Testament has a word for it – *pleonexia* – an unnatural irrational itch for more. It takes many forms – sexual excesses and perversions, the miser's greed, the dictator's love of power – but it is always a monstrous disease of the soul. Desire in us sinners does not always reach such an obviously pathological pitch of enormity. But, nevertheless, it stands in need of redemption.

Then it is the lot of all finite things to be subject to change. Change is the law of life. Like a dancing ball at the apex of a jet of water, the organism is poised at the point where the antagonistic forces of renewal and decay have reached an equilibrium. But the law of life is also the law of death. Sooner or later that equilibrium is lost. The processes of degeneration and decay overcome those that make for renewal, and death supervenes. Like all organisms man is mortal. What is characteristically human in him is not his mortality but his consciousness of it – not that he changes

but that he knows this and rebels against it. It is his rampant
desires that makes his experience of change so poignant. He
finds it hard to reconcile himself to getting old. When his
body loses its suppleness, when his mental powers are no
longer equal to the demands he makes upon them, when his
memory fails and his eyes grow dim – then his consciousness
of change awakens the sense of mortality in him. And if his
dominant desires have been for things that, being finite, are
themselves subject to change and destruction, the man suffers
inevitable loss and frustration. The flowers he risked his life
to pluck have withered. And sometimes he feels a still sharper
pang – when the change is not in the things he desired, but
in him. The precious stones for which he bartered his soul
still flash their fire for other eyes, but for him they are now
dull, worthless pebbles. To sell all we have to buy the
world's treasures and then to find that we no longer desire
them or take any pleasure in possessing them – that is the
very torment of hell. For we have come to our senses too late.

Too late! For now we have to take note of yet another
aspect or dimension of our finite, human experience – its tem-
porality. 'Time, like an ever-rolling stream, bears all its sons
away.' And on that stream there is only one-way traffic. The
present flows away into the past and never returns. Opportunities of doing good that we have lost never recur. Other
opportunities may come our way, but we ourselves are
changed. *We* do not recur. The self that heard but did not
heed the Word of God, that saw but left unhelped a
neighbour's evil plight – that self is dead for ever. In its place
is another self, the same yet not the same, like it yet different
– a self changed and hardened by that refusal of divine grace,
that unwillingness to respond to human need.

Though the past is beyond recall, the evil we did, the good
we left undone, these linger in our memory and fill us
with remorse. How can I forget the devastation wrought in
other lives by my callous selfishness? Asks Macbeth of the
physician –

154

Canst thou not minister to a mind diseas'd,
Pluck from the memory a rooted sorrow,
Raze out the written troubles of the brain,
And with some sweet, oblivious antidote
Cleanse the stuff'd bosom of that perilous stuff
Which weighs upon the heart?

And the doctor replies –
        Therein the patient
    Must minister to himself.

But what if the patient cannot minister to himself? Unless memory can be redeemed annihilation is the best we can hope for. For the bitter recollection of the past throws its shadow over all the prospect before us. We dread the unknown future. We fear the loss of our loves. We are anxious regarding evils pre-visaged – some half-known, others only guessed at. Even when no definite danger threatens us we are anxious still – then, indeed, more anxious than ever, straining our eyes to penetrate the swirling mist that hides the shape of things to come. We try to forget the bitter past and the menacing future by clutching the present moment as it flies. We snatch at present thrills and turn our backs on the clock whose hands are mounting towards the midnight hour. Or, perhaps, we are in a worse case and find the present empty of all interest and delight. Perhaps we couldn't care less – as we say. But to stop caring is to be in a hell below hell, where not even the fiercest torments can break the sleep of eternal death.

Finally, it belongs to our finitude that we cannot be complete persons apart from our fellows. Our human personality is as much a product as an ingredient of community. We human beings are naturally sociable creatures. We need one another, and cannot be truly human in isolation. Solitary confinement is the most terrible punishment that can be inflicted on us. 'That way madness lies.' It is only by joining in the rough and tumble of community life that we learn to be persons – whether that community be the family, the school, the village or the wider community of the nation. But although we cannot do without other people, it sometimes seems that we cannot do with them either. Temperaments clash, interests conflict. We get on one another's nerves. We are often cruel and unjust to our neighbours. We forget that they are persons in their own right and want to treat them as things – tools to be used for our own selfish ends. Once again, it is sin that spoils our finitude. And here, once again, the sin is precisely our unwillingness to accept that finitude – our reluctance to comply with the conditions on which alone our full humanity can be achieved. And so chaos and anarchy menace the entire range of those social relationships which are the field of our personal fulfilment. We need our neighbours, yet find it hard to be neighbourly. We can be real persons only by admitting other persons into our lives, yet too often we shut them out.

Here, too, we are sinners who come short of the glory of God. Every creature gives glory to God by obeying the law of its nature and so achieving the particular excellence for which God created it. Our particular excellence as human beings is to be true and full finite persons – the loving children of God, made in his image and reflecting his likeness. We give glory to God when we gladly and humbly accept this destiny. We cannot love God without loving our neighbour as ourselves. We cannot be reconciled to him without being reconciled to one another and to our finitude. 'The hope of glory', therefore, looks not to an individual, unshared blessedness – 'the flight of the alone to the Alone' – but to the communion of saints, the perfect heavenly society of the city of God.

Sin in us is our reluctance – or even our refusal – to accept our finitude. But when by the grace of God in Christ the demons of pride and selfishness have been driven out and we sit clothed in humility and in the sanity of loving trust in God and glad obedience to his holy will, then we have received the earnest of eternal life – the first instalment of the redemption of our finitude. 'Beloved, now are we the sons of God, and it doth not yet appear what we shall be . . .' No. We cannot even guess at the unimaginable glories of our future life in the nearer presence of God. Far more is involved in the redemption of our finitude than our earthbound minds can hope to trace. Yet of some things we may have good assurance.

Because we are finite we are, and shall remain, creatures of desire. Here in our blindness and waywardness we have often desired what could not give us true content. We have spent money for that which was not bread, and our labour for that which could not satisfy us. Yet the meaning of our subjection to desire – the ground basis of all our longings, however foolish and selfish – has ever been our longing for God – to see his glory and to rejoice in his love. But this is a desire which in the saints is ever satisfied and ever renewed, a desire that is never frustrated and an enjoyment that never palls. For the wonder of God's being is inexhaustible.

Then because we are finite we are, and shall remain, subject to change. But change itself will be redeemed. No longer will it lead us by a downward path to dusty death, but it will become the law of our finite apprehension of the unchanging Infinite. No more will it bring to our spirits any pang of sorrow, but will enrich us with an unending increment of new delights and deeper joy and purer worship as we contemplate now one, now another facet of the infinitely rich and varied glory of God's being. We ourselves shall be changed indeed, and we shall go on changing. But now change in us will be from glory to glory. Our bodies, too, will be transformed by a death and a resurrection into perfect instruments for doing the Father's will and sharing in the family love and joy of his children.

There can be no continuing identity of personal existence apart from memory. To be the same persons as we are in this life we must be able to recall the past and acknowledge

157

it as ours. But that means that our redemption will not be complete until our memories have been purged of all bitterness of shame and remorse. And purged they will be, by the power of that atonement whereby Christ has reconciled us to God, to one another and to ourselves. In this life we believe – and can only believe – that Christ crucified and risen has made for our sins that full reparation for our wrongdoing that we ourselves can never make. There in heaven we shall not *believe* – we shall *see* that all is well – that where sin abounded, there did grace much more abound. There our consciences will be at peace at last, and we sinners shall be able to forgive ourselves as fully and freely as God has already forgiven us.

In the city of God we shall be complete persons. We shall have found our fulfilment not in selfish isolation from our fellows but in closest communion with them. Yet someone may say: 'No doubt the vision of God's glory will bring us unspeakable joy. But to have to share it with all sorts of queer people, to have to live with them, and put up with them, there as we have to here – isn't that going to be a pretty heavy discount?'

It would be if they and we were to be no different in heaven from what we are here on earth. But we shall all be different. We need to be radically different before we shall be ready to see God's face. And when at last we do see him, we shall also see what he sees, and shall look at our neighbours with his eyes and love them with his love.

We picture heaven as a place. We draw the contrast between earth and heaven in terms of 'here' and 'there'. We speak of the 'present world' and of the 'world to come'. But this 'here' and 'there', 'present world' and 'world to come' are just as much picture language as the pearly gates and golden streets of the book of Revelation. And our pictures mislead us if they make us think of heaven as a world entirely different and separate from the one we now inhabit. Heaven, it is true, seems to us shadowy and insubstantial compared with the world of our everyday lives. This world with its sin and heartbreak seems so tragically solid and real. Yet because Christ died on Calvary and rose triumphant from the grave, this world for all its evils is God's world. And just because it is his world the soul of goodness in it is more real than the evil that afflicts it. For goodness does not pass with the setting of the sun but endures to all eternity. The world passeth away and the lust thereof, but goodness abides, for goodness is what God eternally wills. And our faith may boldly add that 'he that doeth the will of God abideth for ever'.

'The world passeth away.' *The end of the world* is a phrase that bears more than one meaning. The imaginative picture of Jewish Apocalyptic portrays a world consumed by fire after the Lord's people had been snatched away to safety. Our modern imagination, maybe, pictures a lifeless, meaningless universe, like an empty theatre when the play is over and the actors have departed, or like an abandoned ship drifting endlessly through a perpetual night. But is there not some hidden Gnostic dualism lingering here? Is this the best God can do? Is there, after all, waste in his universe? Or perhaps some intractable thing, fit only to be destroyed? Is salvation no more than salvage? Surely not. Salvation is not salvage but fulfilment. Not the snatching of elect individuals as brands from the burning, but a cosmic redemption in which the whole creation shares in the glory of the children of God. 'And I saw a new heaven and a new earth.' That is the New Testament note. The keyword of Christian eschatology is not destruction but transformation. 'Behold, I make all things new.' To be finite is to be doomed to death. But it is the work of grace to make death the gateway to fuller life and to transform our mutability with its frustrations into a means of ever richer and more satisfying existence. The old order passes, and with it the domination of sin and death over our finite years. But God's new order – the Bible teaches us – begins here and now, amidst the ruins of the old dispensation. 'He that believeth hath eternal life.'

There are indeed intimations of immortality – foretastes of heaven – given to us by our loving Father that we may be of a good courage on our pilgrim way. Home is one. Nothing is perfect on earth, but at its best home shines with a heavenly light and quickens within us the hope of glory. For it is at home that we are loved for our own sakes and treated better than we surely deserve to be. We get justice there, for we get sympathy and understanding. We can be and give our best there for each of us has his own place that no one else can take. We belong there and we count. There, too, our hearts are at rest. Of course, there are times when the family is too much for us. The children grow tiresome with their noisy games. 'Oh, run along now,' we say. 'Leave me in peace.' We need times of quiet, yet we know well enough that peace does not come from being left to ourselves. Peace is not solitariness, but the harmony of kindred minds. It is the atmosphere of a happy home.

Friendship, too, gives us a foretaste of heaven. People sometimes ask whether we shall recognize our friends when we get to the other side. That question, I imagine, is prompted by our experience of the way time and distance can weaken friendships here on earth. Letters are a poor substitute for daily meetings and many of us are indifferent correspondents anyway. As the years pass by absent friends grow apart from us. They make new friends and acquire new interests, until they live in a world to which we have no access. When at last we meet again after long years of separation, there is embarrassment on both sides. Time has left its mark on our faces, so that even physical recognition may be difficult. We try to pick up the threads again by going back in memory to the past we have left behind, but it is far from easy. Our memories are blurred. Now we are not estranged from these old friends by any quarrel or misunderstanding. We look back with great pleasure on the years we spent in their society. But our friendship is only the ghost of what it once was. Will it be like that in heaven? Those who pass beyond our sight journey on in lands unknown to us and experience wonders of grace and glory far above the highest sweep of our imaginations. Will they forget us and the love they bore us? Shall we recognize them when at last we see them again?

There is no doubt about the answer. In heaven we shall be nearer to our friends than ever we were on earth. Their resurrection bodies, though glorified and made perfect, will still be *their* bodies. Here on earth misunderstandings arise even between the best of friends – for we cannot always communicate our deepest thoughts or explain the hidden reasons for our actions. Yet even here are moments of unforgettable communion when without a word spoken we read the thoughts of our friends and share their inmost life. There all misunderstandings will have disappeared. We shall know one another better than we do now, for we shall have a deeper and more intimate knowledge of Christ who stands at the centre of all our personal relationships and is the best interpreter of what our hearts would say to one another. The moments of richest fellowship in this life are not to be compared with the full glories of the communion of saints. Yet here, too, we have a foretaste of heaven. We have been made members of Christ's Body – the Church. When Christ makes us his friends he breaks down the barriers that divide us from each other. At first we do not realize what is happening. And sometimes we are slow to learn that we cannot have Christ without being willing to share him with everybody else. We admit it in theory, no doubt – but when it comes to treating people of other races and colours, yes, even members of other Christian churches – as friends of our Friend to whom he opens his mind and gives his confidence just as he does to us – why, that is another thing altogether. Yet, for all our faults and our slow progress in Christ's school, the Church does give the world a foretaste of heaven, and more than a hint of what it will be like when Christ's friends are all made one in mutual love and perfect equality.

'I saw no Temple therein.' In Jerusalem the Golden there is no cathedral, no building set apart for the worship of God, for the entire city is a worshipping community and all its streets resound with praise. In that worshipping community we and those we love may be united on earth and reunited in heaven. To be at home in the city of God, to see God's face and do him service in tasks where toil refreshes our spirits like perfect rest – this is our life's fulfilment and reward. This is the hope of glory.

Heaven and Hell

A. M. RAMSEY

When I was honoured by the invitation to visit New College and to give the Drew lecture my mind turned quickly to the names of some of the great teachers of theology who belonged to the College in the past. To one of these my own debt is immense – Peter Taylor Forsyth. It is hard to think of a theologian who exhibited so thoroughly as he the central place of the Cross in Christianity. He was concerned as a teacher with many of the great Christian doctrines, but he saw all of them in the light of that relation of sinful man and holy God which the Cross discloses. To him heaven was the adoration of the Lamb as it had been slain.

When once I had chosen Heaven and Hell as my subject I turned for help to the writings of Forsyth. And not in vain, for I lighted upon this arresting passage:

> Prayer is the nature of our hell as well as our heaven. Our hell is ceaseless, fruitless, hopeless gnawing prayer, prayer which cannot stop, prayer which is addressed to nothing, and obtaining nothing. And prayer is our heaven. It goes home to God, and attains there and rests there.[1]

These words are puzzling, and it is *after* we have wrestled with our subject that their meaning may come home to us. So I will return to them later. Yet at once the words convey this to us, that heaven and hell, far off though they be, are related closely to the here and now, giving intensity to the present moment.

It would be easy in speaking about heaven and hell to wander into doctrines which stand near to them in the

Christian scheme, such as the doctrine of the Communion of Saints with its bond of the living and the departed in mutual prayer and praise, or the doctrine of the state of those who have died in faith. Let me mention in this connexion only that it seems clear that, when our Lord told the dying thief that he would be with him that day in paradise and when St Paul spoke of death as to depart and to be with Christ, the implication is plain that the departed are in a state of consciousness and of personal relationship in fellowship with Christ; but it is not to be assumed that perfection or final glory is at once bestowed after death.

But my present task is to consider with you not this intermediate state of grace and patience, pain and joy, but the finalities, heaven and hell. Yet one preliminary theme must needs prepare our way. It is resurrection. The sequence of the Creed reminds us that we should think first about the resurrection of the dead before we think about the life of the world to come. It is upon the Resurrection that the Christian hope is based, and resurrection belongs both to our present state as Christians and to the final destiny.

First, then, resurrection is a mighty act of God. Remember that in the New Testament the language used is not of Jesus rising but of Jesus being raised by God. Jesus did not 'achieve' resurrection. Rather did he make himself nought, and when all was dark, when human possibilities were exhausted, God raised him by a mighty act of his power. This truth about resurrection colours the whole process of man's movements towards his goal, whether in this world or the next. It is not that man, even under God's grace, gets gradually better and better and so attains to saintliness here and to heaven thereafter. Rather does the grace of God work surprises, turning defeats into deliverances, 'calling things that are nought as though they are', and acting beyond any laws of progress or expectation. We have no rights here, and no rights hereafter. Unprofitable servants at every stage, we know that the Christian life has always the two facets: on the one side there is the God who raises the dead and on the other side there is 'faith alone'.

Secondly, the resurrection of Jesus is the prelude to the resurrection of those who believe in him and are united to him by faith and baptism. I need not recall to you the many references to this in the New Testament.[2] Already the Christians united with Christ are raised together with him. Already they are partakers of Christ, possessors of his life-giving Spirit, sharers in eternal life; St Paul and St John are at one in affirming this present realization. But there is a 'not yet', and a consummation still to come. Though they are already 'in Christ' the Christians are still living in this world, they belong to cities, states, and nations. They are involved in suffering, and in sin which contradicts their Christian status. But amid this ambiguous interim they await a future glory. It will be an unveiling in perfection of a union with Christ at present hidden and incomplete. It will be 'the coming of Christ', 'the resurrection', 'the glory'. It must be wrong to try to be literalistic about the imagery used to express the inexpressible, for 'eye hath not seen, nor ear heard, neither have entered into the heart of man, the things which God hath prepared for them that love him.'[3]

Thus through the doctrine of resurrection in the New Testament, with its double strain of something already realized and something 'not yet', we approach the doctrine of heaven. Here let the word 'glory' guide us in our approach. It is one of the marvellous words of the Bible, for it tells of heaven and the last things and it also tells of man and the first things. So it is; God created man in his own image in order that he might come to perfect fellowship with his Creator. It is a fellowship of intimacy, love, and knowledge intermingled with awe and dependence as, for all the intimacy, the line between Creator and creature ever remains. It is this blending of intimacy and dread dependence, of man reflecting the Creator's character and humbly ascribing all to him, which the Bible describes by the words *glory* and *glorify*.

There is the secret of man's existence and of his rôle in the created world, and the clue to man's destiny. Heaven is the final consummation of this, for heaven is man finding himself in the glory of his Maker.

So we approach the thought of heaven. Let me now quote St Augustine, in words rooted in the Bible: 'We shall rest, and we shall see: we shall see, and we shall love; we shall love, and we shall praise. Behold, what shall be in the end, which is no end.'[4]

There is 'a description of heaven'. Let us follow the description through.

'We shall rest.' There is in modern religion a strain of discontent with the idea of heaven as rest. Why, we are told, should repose and inactivity be the goal of energetic men and women? Hence the modern reaction from the phrase 'rest in peace' upon tombstones, and the liking for words like 'called to higher service'. But these modern ideas are not profound, and they belong to a secularized view of religion. How profound in contrast is St Augustine's word *vacabimus:* we shall have a vacation. We shall cease from our restless busyness, from doing things for the sake of doing them; and, purged of the egotisms of our own activity, we shall for once be passive and in our passivity realize that it is God who works. So in this passivity our eyes will be open, and we shall see. *Videbimus*, we shall be freed so as to see God in his perfect beauty, and 'blessed are the pure in heart, for they shall see God'. It will be a vision glorious and satisfying, the goal for which we were created. And as we see God in his beauty we shall begin to reflect him, for the seeing will be in a purity of love whereby his love becomes our own. This reflection of him will mean that we love, love him and all his creatures. *Amabimus*, we shall love our fellows and be serving them selflessly; the second great commandment will be perfectly fulfilled in the realization of the first. Serving our neighbours we shall rejoice in them and with them; and we shall as never before enjoy our fellow creatures. But in the midst of this

166

love, service, enjoyment we shall be aware as never before that God is the giver and God is the goal; and in full circle the heart which has moved from God to creatures will be drawn back to God in praise and wonder. *Laudabimus*, we shall praise God, rejoicing to give to him all that is his due. If the Latin verbs in St Augustine's description have till now served as well as words can serve, here the Latin *laudare* scarcely matches the Greek δοξάζειν, the giving glory to God which is the crown of heaven's meaning. Rest, see, love, praise – each leads on to the other, and all interpenetrate *in fine sed non in fine*, in the end which is no end.

Such will be a perfection in which the contradictions familiar in our present existence are resolved. At present we oscillate between *possession* and *discovery*. We know at times the happiness of arrival and achievement. But this can soon be dulled, and we set out again to find the happiness of the chase, of search, struggle, and exploration. In heaven, however, the joy of arrival and possession and the joy of exploration are one; for while all is perfect there is within perfection a ceaseless discovery of novelty – it is ever a new song that is sung before the throne. So too we experience here the contrast between *rest* and *action*; rest is enjoyable but it can become boring, and so we plunge into activity, but activity after satisfying us awhile can tire us and make us long for rest. In heaven, rest and action are one; the saints rest from their labours, and their works follow them. Our peace is in the will of God, *semper agens, semper quietus*. So too in our present experience we never escape the antinomy between *worship* and *service*. We speak often of their unity, but we know in practice the tension between them. In heaven worship and service are utterly one. There is 'no temple there', for all is worship, and 'his servants shall serve him, and they shall see his face'. Thus will our familiar contradictions disappear in the glory of God.

As heaven is that glory, there can be no idea of it as a selfish compensation for life's frustrations, or as 'pie in the sky when you die'. No selfish desires can lead a man towards heaven as heaven is the very contradiction of selfishness. There is indeed a doctrine of reward in the teaching of Christ. But the good works which win reward are the outcome of God's reign in God-centred lives, and can never be a selfish investment. And the reward to which good works prepare the way cannot be quantitative as it is the reward of being with God in his presence.

The hope of heaven is one aspect of the Christian hope which the New Testament formulates in more ways than one. Besides the hope of heaven there is the hope of the coming of the reign of God in history. The Christians pray 'thy kingdom come on earth as it is in heaven'. Since love is one and indivisible there is no separation between the love wherewith we serve humanity in Christ's name and bear witness to his reign on earth, and the love which is eternal life and the anticipation of heaven itself. Thus we cannot pursue the quest of heaven without a concern about God's reign in history, and equally our concept of God's reign in history will be secularized and robbed of depth if we are negligent of the hope of heaven and our present heavenly citizenship.

Just as we cannot conceive the reign of God in history apart from heaven which is beyond history, so too we are encouraged by scripture and the Christian tradition to think of things terrestrial as not abolished but fulfilled in heaven. That is the significance of the Resurrection of the Body. It does not necessarily mean the *resurrectio huius carnis* understood by some of the Latin Fathers; rather does it mean that there will be in heaven fullness of personal expression, of recognition, and of the characteristics through which people have been known and loved in this present life. *Non eripit mortalia, qui regna dat caelestia.* The doctrine of the *final* resurrection of bodies to complete the beatitude of the saints conveys in symbol the truth that the perfection of the one is inseparable from the perfection of all those who are to be made perfect. The joy of one is incomplete without the joy of all.

Will, however, some be lost? The teaching of Christ in the Gospel of St Matthew ends with a pair of parables of judgement, describing the fate of those within and those without the covenant. The first is the parable of the Talents. It tells of how those who have received gifts will be judged in accordance with their use of them. The second is the parable of the Sheep and the Goats. It tells of how all the nations, the Gentiles outside the covenant, are gathered at a final assize; and they are judged by their response to the natural law of kindness and charity – a response by which, all unknowing, they have been either ministering to Christ or spurning him. 'Inasmuch as ye did it unto these my brethren, ye did it unto me.' We learn from this that those who have had no chance of being confronted with the knowledge and truth of Christ are judged in accord with the light which conscience has given them.

But both of these parables of judgement end with a description of loss, the one describing it as 'outer darkness' and the other as 'the fire of the age to come'. Is there a hell? Can a man, be he a believer or be he an unbeliever, exclude himself from heaven?

The *credibility* of hell rests upon the concept of human freedom. Our freedom is the condition of our human dignity, of our being creatures who are not automata but can will to love or not to love, of our place in a world based upon love and not upon mechanism, of our adherence to an ethical theism. I am free. Rob me of my power to separate myself from the love of God and to shut myself in darkness, and you rob me of the freedom whereby I know myself the child and creature of the holy Father. This exclusion is hell, the self-exclusion of those who prefer to be isolated in self-love because they want it so to be. Theoretically it is hard to see how the loss can be *eternal*, for, as F. D. Maurice insisted, eternity is the quality of God and of the life shared with him. Theoretically, it could be everlasting. But is it? We have to ask what has been *revealed* by Christ.

Christ describes the loss and punishment of those excluded
from him at the judgement, and the adjective in the Gospels
is αἰώνιος which some would translate 'everlasting' and
others of the aeon to come'. We are reckoning with imagery,
and imagery is poetical. We need not be compelled to take
literally the fire and the gnawing worm, nor perhaps the
language of duration. We know that there was a tendency
in the early Church to elaborate the imagery of apocalyptic
in the tradition of the word of Jesus, as a comparison of some
parallel passages in St Mark and St Matthew shows.[5] Yet
when full allowance has been made for sayings which are
poetic rather than literal and for the possibility of elabora-
tions in the gospel tradition, it is impossible to eliminate sayings of Jesus which give terrible warning as to the possibility
of loss and exclusion.[6] Warnings against loss of salvation are
there, incisive and inexorable. What the state of loss may
be like or how many may be lost, we do not know. It is one
of those matters where our Lord seems to give us not defini-
tions, nor answers to our curiosity, but warning and challenge. 'Are there few that be saved?' asks Peter, and our Lord
answers, 'Strive to enter by the strait gate'.[7] We put the warning to ourselves, and we make our own the words:

> King of Majesty tremendous,
> Who dost free salvation send us,
> Fount of pity, thou defend us.
> Think, kind Jesus, my salvation
> Caused thy wondrous Incarnation,
> Leave me not to reprobation.

Heaven and hell are called the last things. But they are
anticipated daily in the here and now. Every act of faith and
charity, every movement of heart and mind towards God
are anticipations of heaven. The Christian Eucharist is a
little sharing in heaven's worship, and the Holy Spirit working in us is the first fruits of the heavenly inheritance, the
power already of the age to come. So too is hell anticipated

whenever men isolate themselves in pride and selfishness and make barriers between one another and their Creator. Our life as Christians is one of conflict and ambiguity; we live under grace and yet sin dies very hard within us. Thus heaven and hell already do battle, and the conflict between them may be raging within our prayers as well as our actions.

So I return to the words of P. T. Forsyth with which I started.

> Prayer is the nature of our hell as well as our heaven. Our hell is ceaseless, fruitless, hopeless gnawing prayer, prayer which cannot stop, prayer which is addressed to nothing and obtaining nothing. And prayer is our heaven. It goes home to God and attains there and rests there.

Now prayer is characteristic of piety, and it is plain enough that to be pious is not necessarily to be near to heaven. As with works, so with piety. There can be good works done with zeal and energy, and yet there can be in them a self-conscious busyness or a possessiveness and patronage which leaves the doer in the bondage of self and far indeed from heaven. There can be piety which dwells upon the man's own spiritual state and his self-conscious enjoyment of it, a piety concerned with its own exterior techniques or its own interior feelings, and the devout man can be far indeed from heaven. Philanthropy and piety alike may be nearer to hell than to heaven. But wherever there are works in which God is present through the humility and charity of the doer heaven is not far off. And wherever there is the prayer of a soul hungry for God and ready amidst its own weakness and failure to be filled with God's own charity, the *vacare* being the gate to the *amare*, heaven is very near. So, not only amid the conflicts of the world but within the soul of the Christian as he prays, heaven and hell struggle together like the twins in the womb of Rebekah, and both are near to us at every moment.

Heaven and Hell

NOTES

1. *The Soul of Prayer*, p. 61.
2. cf. Rom. 6. 1–11; Col. 3.1–4.
3. 1 Cor. 2.9.
4. *De Civitate Dei* xxii. 30.
5. e.g. Mark 13.23–7 and Matt. 24.25–31; Mark 10.29 and Matt. 19.28.
6. See Mark 14.21; Matt. 7.22–3; Luke 13.26–8; Matt. 10.28; Luke 12.5; 13.23–4.
7. Luke 13.24.

172

Immortality and Bereavement

PETER BARRACLOUGH

I could justify my title: 'Immortality and Bereavement' on the grounds that previous Drew lectures have left me little to talk about on the purely theological level. Moreover, when you ask someone in pastoral charge to speak on this theme, his mind naturally turns to those people who are most in need of 'instruction, assurance and inspiration...as to the soul's destiny,' namely: the bereaved.

But I am also aware that I chose this title for more personal reasons. Three times in my life I have suffered close and severe bereavements. Once in the formative years of early adolescence, and twice in quite tragic and harsh circumstances. It is not my intention to thrust the details of these personal griefs upon you; but they inform and colour much of what I have to say. Though I have read many books and papers, this lecture was finally written, and is delivered from the heart. The work of preparing it has involved not only intellectual effort, but also that inner travail of trying to face one's own feelings honestly.

To begin with, I want to affirm my belief in the Christian doctrine of personal immortality. The teaching of Jesus simply assumes that there is life after death. Do I need to bolster that statement with quotations? The parable of the Rich Man and Lazarus; the words to the dying thief; the parable of the Sheep and the Goats: whatever else these things mean, they take it for granted that death is not the end. In particular that death is not the end of our dealings with God, or of his with us. And we cannot say that Jesus took this for granted because everybody else at that time did. We specifically know that this was not so. I am thinking of his

173

controversy with the Sadducees; an influential group, among the Jews of his day, who denied that there is any life after death.

This group directly challenged Jesus. They propounded a neat little problem which assumed that life after death would necessarily involve the same social structures and relationships that we know here on earth. Their hypothetical case showed that in certain instances this would lead to embarrassing situations. I am not concerned with the particular content of their questions. But our Lord replied firmly to them: 'You are wrong, because you know neither the Scriptures nor the power of God.' He dismissed their problem briefly, and then went on: 'But that the dead are raised even Moses showed, in the passage about the bush, where he calls the Lord the God of Abraham and the God of Isaac and the God of Jacob. Now he is not God of the dead, but of the living; for all live to him' (Luke 20.37–8).

Jesus went back to the first books of the Bible because those were the only parts of Scripture that the Sadducees accepted as authoritative. But in doing so he also went back to first principles. The Jews believed, as we believe, that God is concerned about individuals, and calls them into his fellowship and service. We can, in this life, walk with God. Is it credible that he should cease to care about us when we die? No! Abraham, Isaac and Jacob are still in his hands; he is still their God, and they live with him. This is the basis of our Christian thinking about immortality. God is the immortal, the eternal; and we are his.

Jesus believed and taught that there is life beyond the grave. What made this real, vivid and living truth for the disciples and the early Church, was Christ's own resurrection from the dead. I am well aware that the resurrection of Christ was more than a demonstration that death had been conquered – but I cannot understand why anyone should want to ignore this obvious side of it. The resurrection of Christ was the vindication of his whole way of life, and of his death

upon the Cross. It was the completion of his reconciling
work, and showed his victory over sin and all the powers of
darkness. Nevertheless it still seems to me that its initial and
overwhelming impact upon the disciples was, quite simply,
that their Lord was alive. 'Then were the disciples glad when
they saw the Lord' (John 20.20). This joy continued in the
Church. There thrills through every page, and all the
preaching and living of the 'Acts of the Apostles' the radiant
conviction: 'Our Saviour Jesus Christ...has broken the
power of death and brought life and immortality to light
through the Gospel' (2 Tim. 1.10 NEB).

You will not expect me to rehearse the evidence for the
Resurrection. As I am dealing with this in a very summary
fashion, I will content myself with saying that I am convinced that on the first Easter Day the disciples found an
empty tomb, and later encountered the living Lord in new
and radiant form. I had come to believe this before I applied
to enter the ministry. I looked at all the evidence again in
the light of a theological training which in no way minimized
the problems of New Testament criticism. I have reappraised
it in the experience of bereavement and its aftermath, and
I still believe it. No one was able to knock the bottom out
of this astounding message, nor to undermine the confidence
of the early Church, because the tomb really was empty, and
the Lord was with them.

I know that many people in the modern world, and even
in the Church, find this assertion frankly incredible. So for
that matter did many people in the ancient world. It breaks
the whole mould of materialistic assumptions about the world
and human personality. But can our human experience be
contained within this strait-jacket?

While I was still a scientist I studied the literature which
described experiments about Extra Sensory Perception: ESP
for short. They seemed to me to demonstrate that telepathy,
clairvoyance, and precognition really do occur. Across the
years since then a small but growing number of scientists and

philosophers have agreed that this is so. Professor Eysenck, the Professor in Psychology at London University is not noted for his credulity. But on the subject of ESP he has said this:

> Unless there is a gigantic conspiracy involving some thirty university departments all over the world, and several hundred highly respected scientists in various fields, many of them originally hostile to the claims of the psychical researchers, the only conclusion the unbiased observer can come to must be that there does exist a small number of people who obtain knowledge existing either in other people's minds, or in the outer world, by means as yet unknown to science.[1]

A very cautious statement, but significant. Others have gone further.

In 1949 Professor Sir Alister Hardy, FRS, in giving his presidential address to the Zoological Section of the British Association added this epilogue:

> There has appeared over the horizon something which many of us do not like to look at. If it is pointed out to us we say: 'No it can't be there, our doctrines say it is impossible.' I refer to telepathy – the communication of one mind with another by means other than the ordinary senses. I believe that no one who examines the evidence with an unbiased mind can reject it ... It is perhaps unorthodox for a zoologist to introduce such a topic; but I do so for a reason. If telepathy has been established, as I believe it has, such a revolutionary discovery should make us keep our minds open to the possibility that there may be so much more in living things and their evolution than our science has hitherto led us to expect.[2]

Among philosophical teachers of repute Professor C. D. Broad of Cambridge, and Professor H. H. Price of Oxford, have striven to develop a philosophy which took account of these 'psi' phenomena, as they have been called. And Dr Robert Thouless, a Cambridge psychologist has put forward a fascinating hypothesis about the relationship between the personality and the physical brain, based on his belief in both extra sensory perception and also psycho-kinesis: the ability of the mind to influence the movement of small objects.

Many psychologists would say that these faculties, or capacities of the mind are not abnormal, nor confined to a few people. The story of Freud's gradual acceptance of telepathy is a fascinating one. He came to it reluctantly, for his own background was that of nineteenth-century materialistic science. But he felt he could not ignore the evidence for telepathy, and he knew of a number of cases in which the evidence for telepathy between an analyst and his patient seemed strong enough to be beyond doubt. Ernest Jones, Freud's great friend and biographer, was a resolute sceptic. He considered that the acceptance of telepathy would be fatal to psychoanalysis, and he persuaded Freud not to read an essay on 'Psychoanalysis and Telepathy' to the International Congress in 1922. It was not published until after Freud's death, in 1941.

Freud suggested that telepathy may be the original archaic method by which individuals understood each other, but it was pushed into the background by the more efficient methods of communication through the five senses. The older methods, he came to believe, could re-assert themselves under certain conditions.

The other great founding father of modern psychology, C. G. Jung, accepted the existence of 'psi' phenomena wholeheartedly, and thought deeply about them. A quotation from his posthumously published autobiography, *Memories, Dreams, Reflections*, will make this clear, and also lead us back to our main theme.

'Experiments prove,' he writes, 'that at least part of the psyche is not subject to the laws of space and time.'[3] 'If such phenomena occur at all, the rationalistic picture of the universe is invalid, because incomplete . . . and we must face the fact that our world, with its time, space and causality, relates to another order of things lying behind or beneath it, in which neither "here and there" nor "earlier and later" are of importance.'[4]

I have made this digression because it seems to me that when we ask ourselves if it is possible to believe that the dead live on, and that Christ was raised from the dead, we are really asking fundamental questions about the nature of human personality. Are we so tied to the physical body, so entirely contained within it, that nothing can survive its break-up and dissolution? Or is the physical brain and body something which we inhabit and use so that the essential person need not perish when the body breaks down? What I have been saying is that there is scientific, psychological and philosophical evidence to suggest that man transcends the physical body which he inhabits, and even the material universe of which it is a part.

Now it is ironic that during this period when many scientists have been trying to make room in this scheme of things for the human 'psyche', which is the Greek word for soul, many Protestant theologians have been steadily eliminating it. They have told us that it is positively wicked, and certainly unchristian, to talk about the immortality of the soul. We must speak only of the 'resurrection of the body'; and if this gives offence, so much the better!

I must therefore say something about this, although it was the subject of an earlier Drew lecture. The Apostles' Creed says: 'I believe in the resurrection of the body and the life everlasting'; whereas Mr Drew, who established this lecture, preferred the phrase 'personal immortality'. It is commonplace to say that the first is a Hebraic idea, and the second a Greek one. I do not think that you have said the last word about the validity of either concept when you have said that. A simple classification into what is from Jerusalem and what is from Athens settles no issue of Christian doctrine without further argument.

Let me confess that I have never been able to work up much enthusiasm for the controversy over whether Christians believe in 'the immortality of the soul' or the 'resurrection to eternal life'. Provided, and it is an important proviso, that each is used in a Christian context, I make bold to say that they come to much the same thing.

We owe the idea of resurrection to later Jewish thought, which borrowed heavily from the Persians in this matter, so that one ought perhaps to count Zoroaster among our prophets. Jewish thought could only conceive of being forever with God as involving resurrection. They could not imagine a full personal life without a body of some sort, but it is quite clear in Christian thinking that the risen body is not a body of flesh and blood. 'Flesh and blood,' Paul says, 'cannot inherit the kingdom of God' (1 Cor. 15.50). We shall be given a body, 'clothed in a body' his second letter to the Corinthians says, appropriate to the conditions of life in God's eternal Kingdom. It is, says Paul, 'a spiritual body', or again 'a house not made with hands, eternal in the heavens'.

This knocks on the head all crude notions about the various bits and pieces of our earthly remains leaping together to be re-animated. It is a pity that this crude conception is encouraged by the Latin of the Apostles' Creed: which speaks of *carnis resurrectionem* – the resurrection of the flesh. As H. B. Swete insists in his authoritative little book on The Apostles' Creed: 'The form in which this article is cast in the Western Creed is not Biblical.' It is fortunate that the English translation in the Book of Common Prayer at least modifies it to: 'The resurrection of the body', and even more fortunate that we in the Free Churches are not compelled to recite this creed without explanation, twice a Sunday. The Nicene Creed, prescribed in the Prayer Book for use at the Communion Service, is much less open to

179

misunderstanding: 'And I look for the resurrection of the dead, and the life of the world to come.' *He ek nekrōn anastasis* is undoubtedly the New Testament formula, and has mostly been the one used in Christian teaching from the earliest times.

Now if you understand 'resurrection from the dead' to mean that our essential personalities will be re-clothed by God in appropriate spiritual bodies, it is not very different from saying that you believe in the personal immortality of the soul that is related to God and has fellowship with God. Provided of course that you accept that this 'soul' is not a ghost, fated to a ghostly existence, but once again the essential human personality clothed in the spiritual form God has designed it for.

It may seem to some of you that I am very naïve thus to dismiss a protracted and sometimes bitter theological controversy. But I can only say that when I re-read Oscar Cullmann's *Immortality of the Soul or Resurrection of the Dead?* in preparation for this lecture, I felt once again that I had gone all the way round a revolving door, and come out on the same side as I went in. There are interesting and important truths to be seen in the process, but does not Cullmann himself say at the end: 'There is a sense in which a kind of approximation to the Greek teaching does actually take place (in the New Testament), to the extent that the inner man, who has already been transformed by the Spirit (Rom. 6.3ff.), and consequently made alive, continues to live with Christ in this transformed state...'[5]

I return therefore, unabashed, to the point that the classic Christian approach to the conviction of personal immortality is based on the line of thought laid down in Christ's teaching, and clinched by his own conquest of death. Because he lives, we shall live also. But now, from this glorious light, we must be willing to plunge into the darkness. You might assume that if these convictions are firmly held, grief at bereavement will be swept away.

My own personal and pastoral experience suggest that this is not so, and wider reading on the subject of grief and mourning confirm it. Does this surprise you? It is part of my contention in this lecture that we do not take death seriously enough. Christ is risen, and we shall share in his victory; but death remains a grim enemy. 'The last enemy that shall be destroyed is death.'

We must remember that the first disciples expected the Resurrection of Christ to be followed rapidly by the end of all things. Their Lord would return in manifest glory and power, and all would be safely gathered in. Already in the New Testament we find evidence of disquietude when this did not happen. And in particular it would seem that the Christians at Thessalonica were perturbed because some of their number had died before the Lord returned. They had obviously expected that they would all be alive to share in the blessings which would come with the arrival of the Lord 'from heaven'. Paul wrote (1 Thess. 4.13ff.) to reassure them that departed Christians would share equally with those who still lived at the coming of the Lord.

What can we say about the early Christians' expectation of the imminent return of the Lord except that they were wrong? It didn't happen; it hasn't happened. And after nineteen hundred years we cannot really recapture what they felt. We believe that the culmination of history will find Christ to be all in all; but we have to go on living 'between the times' without the ecstatic hope that the Lord will arrive tomorrow, or the next day, and put everything right. This obviously affects the Christian experience of grief. We do not sorrow as those who have no hope; but our hope is very much deferred compared with the early Christian hope. To put it at its mildest, bereavement involves a separation from our loved ones which is more like their going to Australia for the rest of our lives than taking a mere week-end away in Eastbourne.

We are more open to the experience of human grief, and

we cannot use any and every New Testament text to paper over deep chasms of sorrow. I may be wrong about this; but if I am wrong, it will at least act as a corrective. And after all, Jesus wept at the grave of Lazarus his friend. Let not his ministers offer too easy and quick a comfort to the bereaved without understanding, and to some extent sharing in, what they are going through.

Some time ago, I was taking a service at a crematorium for one of my members. I noticed that the front pew, by the catafalque, the pew into which the nearest family mourners are usually put, was roped off, and could not be used. I asked the chapel attendant why, and he took me to the pew and showed me a wide and jagged gap in the wooden beading along the bottom edge of the prayer-desk. 'At an earlier service,' he said, 'one of the mourners was so distraught as the coffin moved from the catafalque that he wrenched off that strip of wood.' You may want to tell me that the frenzied man was not a Christian. I have no idea whether he was or not; but in that splintered wood I saw what human grief is like. And as Christians have we never wanted to clutch at what is passing from us, and pull it back? We may delude ourselves into believing that we feel nothing of this; but we would be wrong.

The death of someone who has played an important and significant part in your life is a shattering experience. Whatever we believe about the after-life, death brings a sharp earthly separation. It has to be faced and its consequences gone through. The whole pattern of our earthly life has been disturbed, and this is painful.

John Hinton, in his book on *Dying* has a chapter on 'Reactions to Bereavement'. He begins it thus:

After a person has died those who knew and loved him continue to suffer. Even if death has been anticipated for a long time, when it finally comes there is a resurgence of grief. The immediate reactions of the bereaved will not

be limited to those of straightforward sorrow. The death
will arouse in them a great turmoil of emotions and give
rise to wide variations in behaviour in different people.[6]

Dr Eric Lindemann published a short paper on 'Symptomatology and Management of Acute Grief' in 1944, based
on the study of a number of bereaved people. He found that
there were five characteristic symptoms which almost always
turned up. I will list them under his brief headings and
comment upon them in my own words.

Somatic distress
That is to say the bereaved frequently experience bodily
symptoms of pain and distress. They develop minor or even
major physical upsets. Many have to visit the doctor more
often than they usually do.

Preoccupation with the image of the deceased
This causes stabs of anguish and yearning at each fresh
reminder of the loss. Tennyson expressed this when he cried
out:

> But O for the touch of a vanish'd hand
> And the sound of a voice that is still!

Some of us know that you can still occasionally feel like that
even a decade after a serious bereavement.

Guilt
Many mourners when they think of the deceased say to themselves, and sometimes to the minister: 'I wish I'd done this
for them,' 'I wish I hadn't said that,' and similar phrases
expressive of regret and guilt. Freud, as we shall see, regarded
such guilt as verging on the abnormal or pathological. He
thought it marked the boundary-line between grief and
melancholia, or depression. It can become pathological, but
I have encountered the expression of guilt-feelings so often

among the bereaved that I agree with Lindemann in listing it as a normal concomitant of bereavement.

Hostile reactions

This may startle us if we have neither encountered nor experienced it, but in the immediate aftermath of bereavement the person concerned is often more irascible than usual. It is as if they were looking for a lost object and cannot find it, and are deeply frustrated. In our Western civilization there may not be a great display of anger and resentment, but they are there. Often the latent hostility is directed towards the doctor, clergyman, or social worker who has been trying to help. This may sometimes be justifiable, but more often it is a displaced anger vented on those who failed to prevent the death; and that of course includes God. I shall return to this later.

Loss of patterns of conduct

The bereaved discovers how large a part of his or her customary daily activity was somehow related to the deceased, and has now lost its significance. There comes a general loss of interest in life. Daily tasks are wearisome, and sleepless nights are common.

We must beware of generalizations. We all have different temperaments and there are varying degrees of bereavement. Provided no bereaved person is going to be worried because they have not experienced some of these things, it is helpful to know that many of the bereaved do. These symptoms occur so often that they can be described as the normal reactions to bereavement. They will pass, in time. They will pass without harming us if we accept rather than deny our sadness. Express as much grief as you genuinely feel. Then we must accept the situation and, as we feel able, begin to work at the task of adjusting ourselves to an environment bereft of the physical presence of our loved one.

What is going on inside the personality to cause all these reactions? In 1917 Freud published a paper called *Mourning and Melancholia* which has dominated psychological thinking about grief and mourning ever since, because it was a classic piece of work. He was concerned to correlate mourning and melancholia. Melancholia is now an obsolete word; we should speak of depression, or depressive illness. Both mourning and depression are marked by painful dejection, loss of interest in the external world, loss of capacity to love, and an inhibition of activity. Freud suggested that depression was particularly characterized by guilt feelings which lowered self-regard to the point of continual self-reproach and self-revilings. We have seen that this is indeed the border-line between normal grief and pathological depression. Both mourning and melancholia, Freud pointed out, are reactions to the loss of a loved person or of a valued concept or ideal.

This explains the work which has to be done in mourning. The loved object no longer exists, or at least it no longer exists in the shape and form we were accustomed to, and so all the libido, that is the mental energy with which our minds invest people and objects, has to be withdrawn from its attachment to this object. Then a struggle arises because we do not easily give up our hold on loved objects or people. So a task has to be carried through, with great expense of time and energy, as we sever the ties which bound us to the lost object or person and reattach the invested energy somewhere else.

Freud wrote: 'Why this process of carrying out the behest of reality bit by bit, which is in the nature of a compromise, should be so painful is not at all easy to explain in terms of mental economics. It is worth noting that the pain seems natural to us. The fact is, however, that when the work of mourning is completed the ego becomes free and uninhibited again'.[7]

I think that I should like to add that the work of mourning

is seldom so thoroughly and cleanly completed. It is not my intention to go into the psychopathology of depression, which is a kind of permanent mourning. But one remark which Freud makes, later in this paper, strikes me as being particularly profound, and relevant to the experience of bereavement. He says that a patient in depression 'may know whom he has lost but not what it is he has lost in them'.[8]

This would seem to me so often true of all our losses that it goes far to explain why we sometimes get stuck in our grief. We know whom we have lost; but not what we have lost in them. In other words the experience of bereavement presses upon, and sometimes cracks open, unconscious regions of the mind which we may previously have ignored. We find ourselves, almost literally, out of our depth.

Now having looked briefly at the symptomatology of bereavement, and even more sketchily at what is involved in the psychological readjustments of mourning, it is clear why a simple flourishing of the doctrine of personal immortality will not meet the needs of the bereaved. This is not to say that such a belief makes no difference. I know from my own experience, and from the experience of others, that it makes a great deal of difference. The one whom we have loved is not completely lost to us. They live with God. Therefore our communion with them is not completely severed, but it has to be transformed, liberated from the physical. It can be experienced only as part of our communion with God. It seems to me that our Lord, very gently, helped the disciples to accomplish something like this in the time between his resurrection and ascension. He weaned them, as it were, from the need for sight and sound and touch. Yet they knew it was true when he said: 'Lo, I am with you alway, even unto the end of the world,' and this also brought a forgiveness which overcame guilt.

Christian faith has much to give to the bereaved but can we hang on to this faith as the tides of bereavement flow over us? When I was discussing some of the characteristic symptoms of bereavement, I mentioned anger and resentment, the hostility which can be directed against those who failed to prevent the death. And I added: this of course includes God.

Marris in his sympathetic book on *Widows and Their Families*[9] comments on the frequent sense of injustice felt by young widows after their husbands' deaths. In a religious person, this is bound to be reflected in their attitude to God. As John Hinton says: 'Rather than turn to God when a loved one dies, a few turn away from him, for if God can permit such a death to occur he will no longer be their God'.[10] This kind of thing has been felt and expressed by strong and notable Christians. I want to illustrate it with one or two quotations which add a specifically religious dimension to the experience of bereavement. This is something which psychological and sociological surveys too often leave out.

Dr Joseph Parker was one of the pulpit giants of the Victorian era, and a great Christian soul. He was minister of the City Temple from its opening in 1874 until his death in 1902. In his autobiography, *A Preacher's Life*, there is a chapter headed 'An Irreparable Loss'. It is concerned with the death of his wife, a woman of outstanding personality, striking beauty, lively charm and intelligence. She was considerably younger than her husband, and died when he was in his sixty-ninth year. We make allowances for Parker's colourful and rhetorical style of writing, and catch the sincerity which throbs through this chapter.

On January 26th, 1899, I entered upon my old age, for at 9.30 that night the life of my life, the heart of my heart ascended to the right hand of God. In her fifty-third year Emma Jane Parker died into the life immortal.

Here then is faith in personal immortality; but what does Joseph Parker go on to say?

In that dark hour I became almost an atheist... I had

secretly prayed God to pity me by sparing her, yet He set His foot upon my prayers, and treated my petitions with contempt. If I had seen a dog in such agony as mine I would have pitied and helped the dumb beast; yet God ... cast me out into the waste wilderness and the night black and starless.

He writes at the end of these autobiographical chapters, which were published in the same year as his wife died:

What the outcome is to be we may not even ask. God has handed me, after fifty years service in His Gospel, the cup of misery ... May not the unbeliever mock and the reviler ask me to join the ranks of resentful hostility? I must wait and wonder and keep silence ... My faith is undergoing crucifixion. To what end I know not. Life seems now – perhaps only for a moment – not worth living ... Tears are to me day and night as my meat and drink, while they say continually unto me, 'Where is now thy God?'

The last three years of his life were clouded by this intense sorrow. He continued his work, but was not the same man. He died in 1902, at the age of seventy-one.

I pass on to the testimony of a more recent Christian. In 1961 C. S. Lewis published, anonymously, a little book called *A Grief Observed*. C. S. Lewis married late in life and after a few blissful years his wife died of cancer. He began to jot down his feelings in some old exercise books that he found lying about the house, and recorded the effect of his grief on his religious belief.

No one ever told me that grief felt so like fear. I am not afraid, but the sensation is like being afraid. The same fluttering in the stomach, the same restlessness, the yawning. I keep on swallowing ... At other times it feels like being mildly concussed. There is a sort of invisible blanket between the world and me. I find it hard to take in what anyone says. Or perhaps hard to want to take it in. Yet

I want the others to be about me. I dread the moments when the house is empty. If only they would talk to one another and not to me.[11]

Meanwhile, where is God? This is one of the most disquieting symptoms...A door slammed in your face, and a sound of bolting and double bolting on the inside. After that, silence. You may as well turn away...The same thing seems to have happened to Christ: 'Why hast thou forsaken me?' I know. Does that make it easier to understand?[12]

C. S. Lewis came through that experience. I will not say that he 'got over it', for he himself pointed out that the phrase is ambiguous: 'To say the patient is getting over it after an operation for appendicitis is one thing; after he's had his leg off it is quite another'.[13] I agree. We do not 'get over' bereavement; we go through it, and come out changed. C. S. Lewis wrote one more book: *Letters to Malcolm, Chiefly on Prayer*, and it strikes me as being a calmer, quieter, deeper book than his earlier writings.

Both these men, Joseph Parker and C. S. Lewis, were exceptional. Their bereavements are not typical; for they had invested so much of themselves in one other person, who was taken from them. Yet in the nature of their reaction, and the way it threatened to distort, if not to destroy their faith, we see something which operates in all bereavement.

The experience of bereavement involves us not only in a psychological crisis but also in a crisis of faith. It has theological significance. We cannot just take the death of a person as we take the falling leaves of autumn. Whatever may be true of the biological, in the personal realm death is experienced as an enemy. When someone close to us dies, we feel in ourselves the onslaught of that enemy. The difference between C. S. Lewis writing in 1940 *The Problem of Pain*, and C. S. Lewis in 1961 writing *A Grief Observed*, is the difference between a man studying a War Office manual on infantry manœuvres, and that same man under fire in a real war. Bereavement brings home to us our own mortality. We realize that death is not something that just touches others and leaves us alone. We, and those whom we still have and love, are vulnerable too.

Now when you have realized this, you can do one of two things. You can learn the trick of withholding your heart. Once bitten, twice shy. You can refuse to invest your love in others, who will die; but to do this is to cease to live. It is to turn in upon oneself, and petrify. Or you can open your heart to love, and life, knowing that in doing so, you are opening your heart to pain and death. You will accept that in this world there is no possibility of joy without the possibility of sorrow. We cannot have love, if we refuse suffering.

Joseph Parker cried out: 'My faith is undergoing crucifixion.' What else do you expect to happen to faith and love? C. S. Lewis in his own experience of dereliction said: 'The same thing seems to have happened to Christ... Does that make it easier to understand?' No, it doesn't make it easier to understand, but it makes it possible to bear it, and to believe that God is holding on to us when we can no longer hold on to him.

When I was a theological student preparing for the ministry, we were often told: 'On Good Friday don't forget Easter. On Easter Day don't forget Good Friday. You can't preach the crucifixion without the resurrection. You mustn't preach the resurrection without the crucifixion.' I have certainly discovered that you cannot give a lecture on 'Immortality and Bereavement' without coming face to face with Christ: crucified and risen.

And the risen Lord has still upon his hands and his feet the imprint of the nails, and in his side the wound of a spear. This is how we recognize him as the Lord of Love, and know that nothing in life or death can separate us from God's love in Christ. So even in the darkness we give thanks, because there is light at the end of the tunnel, and the light is eternal. As George Fox wrote in his Journal after a period of heavy inward sufferings: 'I saw also that there was an ocean of darkness and death, but an infinite ocean of light and love, which flowed over the ocean of darkness. And in that also I saw the infinite love of God; and I had great freedom.'

NOTES

1. *Sense and Nonsense in Psychology*, Penguin, 1957, pp. 131–2.
2. Quoted Rosalind Heywood, *The Sixth Sense*, p. 13.
3. op. cit. p. 282.
4. op. cit. p. 283.
5. op cit. p. 56.
6. *Dying*, Pelican, 1967, p. 167.
7. *Mourning and Melancholia*, p. 154.
8. op. cit., p. 155.
9. Routledge and Kegan Paul, 1958.
10. John Hinton, op. cit. p. 169.
11. C. S. Lewis, op. cit. p. 7.
12. op. cit. p. 9.
13. op. cit. p. 43.

Ultimate Triumph

CHARLES S. DUTHIE

It is a matter of agreement among Christians that there shines throughout the New Testament writings the bright hope, the clear assurance that in the long run, however long the run, God will triumph. He will achieve the fulfilment of the purpose disclosed in Jesus Christ. In that consummation God himself, in the phrase of Paul, will be 'all in all'. But as soon as we affirm our belief in this final victory, an inevitable question raises itself in our minds. Will that triumph be complete? Will all who have been fashioned in the image of God be united with him within the redeemed community? Or will some persist obstinately for ever in the repudiation of his grace, self-excluded from heaven? If God wills that all men shall be saved, if he was truly in Christ reconciling the world to himself, if it is his purpose to gather up all things in Christ, are we not driven towards the ex- pectation, perhaps even the certainty, that at the last all shall have found their way, or been led, to God 'who is our home'?

This old question, which we cannot silence, is the question which I propose to consider in this essay. I think it is worth while pausing, at the outset, to note that the question springs neither from a perverse spirit of speculation nor from a desire to evade the reality of God's judgement upon sin. According to Professor Farmer, whose opinions on the subject we shall consider in a moment, it arises 'out of the whole Christian message concerning God and man, and out of the necessities of that new life of trust in God and love to men to which the Christian is called by that message'.[1] I believe this to be a true statement, and I think its truth can be illustrated by a brief preliminary appeal to what we may call the witness

192

of the Christian heart, to the testimony of Scripture and to some recent emphases in Christian theology which base themselves upon the examination of that testimony.

When I have been discussing the final destiny of men with other Christians and especially with those who feel that they must give the fullest weight to the words of Jesus which point to a continuing separation from God in the world to come – such as 'Depart from me' (Matt. 25.41) – I have been prompted to ask the question: 'Granted that the offer of the Gospel confronts man with a momentous choice and that the rejection of this offer may entail precisely this ongoing separation from God, both in this world and in the next, when you look honestly into your own heart, remembering God's gracious dealing with you and his purpose of good for the whole race – do you or do you not entertain the hope that somehow, in the end, all men, even the worst, will be reconciled with him?' Sometimes the answer has been given with reluctance; often it has been qualified; but almost without exception it has been 'Yes, I do cherish that hope.' Please note that the question was asked in order to elicit a true report on what I have called the feeling of the Christian heart. Although the last word cannot be with the Christian heart, what the Christian heart feels in this and in other matters must have *some* importance, since it is itself in some measure shaped by the Spirit of God. I am aware that many Christians might give a different answer to the question, might say, 'I do not cherish that hope', although I should find it hard to believe the evidence of my ears; but I should maintain that the other answer – 'I do cherish that hope' – gives expression to something authentically and deeply Christian. Its significance, I suggest, is to be found, first, in the *possibility* that it springs from a spirit so subdued and permeated, despite its sinfulness, by the wonder of the seeking love of God that it finds it intolerable to contemplate the final exclusion of any from the enjoyment of that love: and, second, that it is conjoined with a due awareness of the fact that a man may continue to flout and to resist that love, with dreadful consequences both here and hereafter. In other words it is not so much universalism as a Christian dogma or philosophy that needs to be examined as the tension between the universalistic element and another weighty factor within the Christian consciousness.

This witness of the Christian heart, a finger pointing to what our fathers called 'the larger hope', would count for little unless it found support in Scripture either in specific statements or promises about a salvation from which none will be shut out or in the vision of what Nels Ferré calls 'the largest logic of God's sovereign love'.[2] We are going to look at the biblical testimony in a moment: let it suffice at this point to say that the passages in the New Testament which suggest a universal restoration must be brought into collision with those which speak plainly of heaven and hell so that the divergence is registered and then fully pondered. The tension in the Christian consciousness of which we have spoken will then be seen as a reflection of a tension already present in the determinative Christian documents. But there is a third witness to which we may appeal in this preliminary attempt to establish the fact that preoccupation with the question of universal salvation arises out of the highest Christian concern. This is the modern emphasis of biblical theology on the racial, indeed the cosmic sweep of Christ's ultimate triumph. It was the world which God so loved that he gave his only begotten Son. It was to create and constitute a new humanity that Christ came. Little wonder that Paul's language rises to lyrical splendour when he comes to speak of the consummation of the divine purpose. Every knee is to bow and every tongue confess that Jesus Christ is Lord, to the glory of God the Father (Phil. 2.10, 11). It is possible that we unconsciously restrict the wide outreach of the apostle's thought because in the order of being we are accustomed to place God first, the world second, the Church third. But for Christians there is a good sense in which the Church comes second and the world after it. If you will allow the language, the Church is God's great idea and the world comes into being to give it visible embodiment. Something very like this seems to be the purport of what Paul writes to the Ephesians and Colossians. Inevitably we are led to ask whether a triumph of the Kingdom that is cosmic and complete will embrace all men. If all are finally subject to God, will all be *willingly* subject to him?

With this introduction I propose to devote the main part of my lecture, first, to considering – and necessarily with selective brevity – what the New Testament has to say on this subject: second, to examining the views of two very dissimilar Christian thinkers of today who tend towards universalism: and, third, to offering some general comments on our theme, as it affects Christian preaching and the Christian life.

As we consider the New Testament, let the teaching of Jesus and the letters of Paul be the main focus of our attention, with a glance at the Fourth Gospel and other writings. In the Synoptic Gospels our Lord leaves his hearers and us in no doubt about the fateful character of our choices here on earth. Let me cite the words of Baron von Hügel:

> We not only find certain texts in the Synoptic Gospels which directly teach Hell and which put it in simple parallel with Heaven; but (an even more conclusive fact) we can clearly trace, through our Lord's teachings, the keen conviction, and the austere inculcation of the conviction, that the spiritual life is a great all-important alternative and choice – a choice once for all, with consequences final and immense.[3]

Thus von Hügel can speak of a doctrine of Abiding Consequences which simply cannot be expunged from our Lord's teaching. This seems to leave us with heaven and hell – although for von Hügel, as for Roman Catholics in general, that cannot be the whole story. Is there no arrow pointing towards universal salvation? In his book *The Bible Doctrine of the Hereafter,* Dr Ryder Smith maintains that there are only two textual pointers, neither of them very clear. The first is contained in the opening clauses of the Lord's Prayer. 'So long', he writes, 'as any sinner, whether man or devil, remains, God's name is not being hallowed, his Kingdom has not come, his will is not being done "as in heaven, so on earth" and God has failed to answer his children's perennial prayer.' The other is the parable of the Leaven, with its suggestive phrase 'till the whole be leavened'. This is indeed very little. Some might perhaps be prepared to infer or to conjecture universalism from the character of God as depicted and demonstrated by Jesus himself as the unwearying seeker of his lost children. Even so, the evidence on the other side has the stronger appearance.

When we turn to Paul we are immediately impressed by his awareness of human responsibility and the fearfulness of the judgement and wrath of God. It is possible for men to perish. Even the security of the new life in Christ demands watchfulness. The treasure is in earthen vessels that the excellency of the power might be of God and not of us. This strain of thought is in direct continuity with the teaching of Jesus. There are, however, several passages which suggest, although they do not explicitly affirm, the possibility that all will be saved. There is 1 Corinthians 15.24–8 where the end will bring all things under Christ's rule and he himself be subject to his Father, when God will be all in all. There is Ephesians 1.20–23 where the authority of Christ subsequent to his ascension and his filling all in all may prefigure and anticipate his complete lordship at the end. There is Ephesians 4.8–10 in which Christ ascends up far above all heavens that he might fill all things. Not least there is the magnificent description in Philippians 2 of the coming triumph of the Christ who took upon himself the form of the servant. One must be careful not to extract too much from these passages. In several of them, and particularly in the last-mentioned, Christ's lordship may be acknowledged unwillingly by some. As von Hügel puts it, the final order might be an order 'which includes the subjection but not the salvation of the godless'. Moreover, there is a lack of precision, an indefiniteness about Paul's language in all the passages I have mentioned which precludes us from asserting more than the final victory of Christ. Whether that victory includes the willing return of all men to God is a larger question which would have to be debated on wider ground. The most that can be said is that these passages are moving in the direction of a universal restoration.

A similar pattern is found in the Fourth Gospel. The purpose of Christ's coming is the redemption of the whole world: 'I came not to judge the world but to save the world' (12.47). John describes him as 'the lamb of God which taketh away the sins of the world' (1.29). In the high priestly prayer Jesus asks that his disciples may be truly one 'that the world may believe that thou didst send me' (17.21–3). But the purpose of God may be thwarted. Men may prefer darkness to light. Christ can say: 'Whither I go, ye cannot come' (7.34). Everlasting life is for believers and the alternative is perishing. The contrast appears most powerfully in a passage such as John 3.16–21 in which the very positive announcement of God's love for the world and his will to save it only brings out more sharply the implicit possibility that some may refuse to believe and thus fail to 'enter into life'. We may mention finally the important statement: 'Now is the judgement of this world. Now shall the Prince of this world be cast outside. And I, if I be lifted up from the earth, will draw all men unto myself' (12.31f.) – from which it *might* be possible to deduce if not the salvation of all, at least the salvation of all *men*. But the evidence is slight; and here again we must conclude, first, that there is but the beginning of a movement towards universalism; and, second, that this is set within the dominant New Testament pattern of two opposed destinies between which men must choose. When we survey the New

Testament as a whole it is the contrast between these two destinies that strikes us first. Von Hügel's idea of 'abiding consequences' is unmistakably present, taking its most arresting form in the Epistle to the Hebrews, the book that dwells so tenderly on the humanity of our Lord and denies, almost savagely, the possibility of renewal and return to those who have denied their faith and crucified the Son of God afresh. In particular, as a recent writer has said, 'it is impossible to deny that there is a doctrine of "everlasting punishment" in the New Testament.' The notion of a universal salvation is tentative and subordinate and to be read almost between the lines. Yet it is present in sufficient strength to generate the tension to which our attention was previously drawn. That tension increases when the argument passes beyond the examination of proof-texts and passages to the consideration of the character of God as holy love, his reconciling action towards man in Christ and the scope of his final triumph.

It is to this wider context that I now wish to turn by bringing into view the opinions of two contemporary theologians who may be said to incline towards universalism without roundly affirming it in so many words. They are H. H. Farmer and Karl Barth. I have chosen these two thinkers because their understanding of the relation between God and man can hardly be said to coincide. If they are nevertheless found moving towards the same conclusion, then we are justified in asking whether there is not some common conviction or insight, above and beyond their differences, which accounts for this movement.

In all his books, Farmer has sought to expound what he calls the massive and consistent personalism of the Christian faith. In his earlier work, *The World and God*, he set forth the thesis that God confronts man in Christ in absolute demand and final succour, so that a personal response must be made out of the freedom and relative independence which man has been granted. The essence of personal, creaturely being is the capacity to say 'Yes' or 'No' to God: without this ten-

sion the structure of true personal relationship is destroyed.
It follows from this that men may persist eternally in rejecting the love of God. But at this point, says Farmer, we are
bound to ask whether a limit is not set to man's abuse of
his own freedom in rejecting God by what he calls the 'un-
qualified universality' of the love of God. *If* all men are to
be saved in the end, this could only happen because God
would have found some way of overcoming the resistance
of the recalcitrant without destroying the freedom from
which their recalcitrance springs. That way is the way of gracious, persuasive, patient and utterly self-giving love.

In a brief but pregnant section of his later book, *God and
Men*, Farmer faces the question of universalism openly. He
begins by seeking to recapture the sense of wonder aroused
by the reality of God's love, the divine Agape. God's love,
he tells us, is such that it 'never turns aside from or deserts
any human person that he has made'. 'On the contrary,'
Farmer writes, 'he seeks with undeviating patience and at
any cost to bring every man back to that true personal life
which is to be found only in fellowship with himself and in
the doing of his will.'⁴ Does this mean that the Divine Lover
will be successful in his pursuit of *all* his errant children? We
are certainly bound to ask very seriously whether it could
be accounted anything other than a most grievous defeat for
God 'if vast numbers of persons are finally lost in some sort
of Hell, or (as some have suggested), by total annihilation'.⁵
But there are several considerations, Farmer goes on, that
make us hesitate to embrace a doctrine of the restoration of
all too easily or too quickly.

The first is the consideration that the reality of human freedom seems to carry with it the possibility of a never-ending rejection of God. There *may* be human spirits who hold out
against God for ever. Universalism might attempt to meet
this in two ways. First, it could maintain that in his infinite
wisdom and love, God might so work upon the unreconciled
that, as we may put it, resistance would no longer be possible.

There would come a willing acknowledgement of and surrender to the God of grace. Moreover, since God has already
overcome the resistance of those who have been reconciled
to him without infringing or destroying *their* status, there
can be no objection to extending this principle to others.
Universalism would then become the theology of the single
decree.

The second consideration that makes us hesitate to tread
the path of universalism, according to Farmer, is the misgiv-
ing that it may take the note of urgency out of Christian
preaching. To which Farmer thinks the universalist might
answer that the man who says he understands a salvation
that has been secured at infinite cost and continues to indulge
himself on the ground that he will be saved in the end, shows
precisely that he understands neither the love of God nor
the meaning of salvation. Moreover, to argue that without
the fear of everlasting damnation there can be no urgency
in the preaching of the Gospel *is to neglect the immediate and
intrinsic urgency of the claim made by God and neighbour.* Finally,
the fact that God will save all does not absolve me from the
responsibility of preaching the Gospel. Both here and hereafter men cannot be saved without their own consent, for
salvation is not something done upon them as inert persons
but a process in which they are intimately involved.

In the third place, Farmer believes, we may be halted in
the journey towards universalism by the sobering thought
that much in the New Testament points in a quite different
direction. We summed this up earlier in von Hügel's phrase
– 'the doctrine of abiding consequences'. This does not quite
shatter the universalist case, Farmer finds. Even if many New
Testament passages indicate that some may be lost, this need
not mean that they actually will be lost.

We may suppose that in creating an order of free persons
God took the risk of Hell, but that it is within the compass
of His manifold wisdom and sacrificial love to circumvent

the risk and save all, as we must believe in fact he has saved some.[6]

There are, too, other passages which suggest or imply a restoration of all men to God. Farmer concludes by making the point that the bare idea of such a restoration is not an adequate description of the final consummation. 'It will be a restoration,' he goes on, 'which contains within it both an infinite cost to God and also the unimpaired significance of human choices and decisions in time.'[7] Meanwhile the crucial confrontation of the soul with Christ is still our task. We are not in a position to say whether anyone ever has or ever will reject Christ finally. We commit everyone in trust to God the Father. We must live in faith with the tension between our conviction that God's love must ultimately prevail and our knowledge of the fatefulness of our human choices and decisions for and against God in this life.

Even from so brief a summary as I have given it must be clear that Farmer's inclination towards universalism never loses sight of the full reality of human freedom. Some theologians would not be prepared to grant to man as much as he does, but the affirmation of such freedom is basic to the whole structure of Farmer's thought. This means that the ultimate coerciveness of God's love is personal, not mechanical. But this insistence on human freedom which may continue to resist God only serves to bring out the more clearly where Farmer rests the weight of his argument. *It is upon the character of God and the ultimate irresistibility of his grace.* I am using the latter phrase deliberately, despite the unhappy associations which cling to the words 'irresistible grace'. It is one thing to say that grace can be resisted and another thing to say that it can be resisted for ever. For Farmer this ultimately irresistible grace is nothing other than the gracious, personal God who meets us in Jesus Christ, as indeed it was for his great teacher, John Oman. In this his thought is not so far removed from that of Karl Barth who rejects the possibility of any decree that comes from a depth in God that lies beyond Christ and anchors election firmly in Christ himself. The second comment I wish to make on the course of Farmer's discussion is that he has shown that belief in universal salvation can still reckon seriously with the gravity of sin. This emerges at two points. The first is his insistence on the reality of the 'wrath of God' which he describes as 'the burning heart of utterly pure love'. The second is the awareness that sin is only met by God at utmost cost to himself and that this costingness continues until the last sinner has been reconciled. Farmer never fails to sound the note of deep moral seriousness.

When we turn from Herbert Farmer to Karl Barth we are made immediately aware of the gigantic nature of the task of assessing his theology, even in what may be considered the limitation of its bearing on a particular problem. Nevertheless it is not difficult to detect a tendency, a direction, a continuing basic concern within his thought. We may begin by noting that Barth's understanding of the relation between God and man does not permit him to follow Farmer in his mode of speaking about human freedom. For Barth what we describe as our freedom is a concept too often framed outside the orbit of grace. It presupposes a power that man has in himself to respond to God and leads to that synergism which is constantly reappearing within the Church to undermine the Gospel by making man partially his own saviour. Man is God's creature. Through grace, in the activity of faith, hope and love 'he responds, he corresponds to what is simply the Work of God for him and to him, the Word of God spoken to him and concerning him'.[8] This unwearied emphasis of Barth must be given its full value before we dare criticize it. Its theme is the glory of grace. But when we have recognized this, we must take serious account of the fact that for the New Testament writers there is a responsive, active element in faith which seems integral to personal relationship with God and which never leads to the notion that man is, with God, his own co-saviour. If this responsive, active element is not rooted, at some point, in human freedom, it is difficult to understand why the apostolic writers feel it necessary to warn their Christian readers of the peril of falling away or indeed why they should have preached for an answer to the offer of the Gospel. The failure of Barth to acknowledge that the human self is genuinely involved, without thereby acquiring merit, in its own salvation by virtue of its God-given, responsible freedom makes it easier for him, as we shall see, to speak of the great decision as already having been taken by God in that self-revelation in Christ which is both election and reconciliation. A path is opened up towards universalism, but unlike the path taken by Farmer, it does not have to surmount the obstacle of a freedom which may express itself in obstinate and persistent disobedience.

To see how Barth's theology moves towards a universalist position, even if it stops short of it, we need to see the importance of election for all his thought. Election for him is a joyful and comforting doctrine because it is that primal decision of God about man which meets us in Jesus Christ. It means that God is for man, not against him. A system in which election and reprobation, as the two sides of double predestination, are in balance with each other simply hides the good news and breeds fearfulness and uncertainty. Christ is the mirror and the foundation of election as in himself the electing God and the elect man. Here indeed we can speak of a double predestination but only with regard to Christ and his suffering. He is the bearer of the Divine No as well as of the Divine Yes, for he who is the elect man is also for our sakes and in our place the rejected man. The fundamental thing is, first that the election is a universal election and, second, that what Barth calls the divine direction and decision have already taken place in this election. Thus the revelation of God's love 'embraces *realiter* both the world and the community, non-Christians and Christians. But the knowledge and proclamation of it is a matter only for the

Christian community.'[9] It would be an embarrassment to
the Christian to be part of this vanguard of humanity if he
did not feel impelled to hope as strongly for those who have
not yet entered into the knowledge of God as he hopes for
other Christians and himself.

Whatever be the vulnerable points of Barth's theology of
election, it cannot be doubted that he has striven mightily
to lift the dark shadow that has lain so long upon this
thoroughly biblical idea. One can only use the word vision
to describe his unfolding of this vast new perspective. Why
is it, notwithstanding, that we cannot rest in it? It is not
because Barth speaks of election as universal. That is only
to say in other words what Farmer says when he speaks of
the love that goes out to all, is concerned for them as they
are and cannot desert them into whatever corruption or sin
they may come. It is rather because he seems to regard the
primal decision of God as having so settled the issue of human
destiny that the significance of a human 'Yes' or 'No' to God's
claim has now scarcely a meaning. The difficulty of establishing the No is proved by Barth's refusal to give sin a status.
He can even speak of the 'ontological impossibility of sin',
of sin existing only on the left hand of God. The difficulty
of establishing the Yes appears from the following passage:

> The decision and act of man are, of course, required by
> the direction given and revealed in Jesus Christ. But the
> requirement of the divine direction is based on the fact
> that in Jesus Christ man has already been put in the place
> and kingdom of peace with God. His decision and act,
> therefore, can consist only in obedience to the fact that
> he begins and does not cease to breathe in this place and
> Kingdom, that he follows the decision already made and
> the act already accomplished by God, confirming them
> in his own human decision and act; that he for his part,
> chooses what has already been chosen and actualised for
> him.[10]

That single word 'only' shows how Barth is still struggling against synergism, any endeavour to put what man has to do on the same level with what God has done. But this language is unauthentic. Is it not plain from the whole Bible, first, that God calls for a decision from man and, second, that the one thing God cannot do for man is to make man's decision *for* God on man's behalf? Berkouwer, the Dutch theologian, is surely right when he says that Barth's 'opposition to all synergism has brought him to the verge of the apokatastasis.'[11] If election in Christ is universal and if in election God has already taken the great decision, it seems difficult to halt on this verge. Nevertheless Barth does halt. Instead of moving to the full universalist position, he brings in the preaching and witnessing task of the Christian community. Let me quote a relevant passage from the *Church Dogmatics*.

The last word in the matter, both in theory and in practice, is that it is their concern, their task, their responsibility to shine as light in the darkness, to proclaim Him to others as the eternally living one, even to those who do not seem to know Him as such. It is one thing to be unreservedly in earnest today about the possibility of eternal damnation for some, and to rejoice equally unreservedly tomorrow at that of eternal reconciliation for all. But it is quite another (and this is the task of the Christian community) to know that one is responsible for attesting with the Christian word and the Christian existence (and the existence no less clearly than the word) Jesus Christ not only as the Lord but also as the Saviour of the world and therefore its future. Christians will never find that they are called to anything other than hope – for themselves and the world. If they were, they would find that they were called to look and to move forward to someone or something other than the Saviour. But then *eo ipso* they could be no longer Christians.[12]

Now the fact that Barth's thought is moving in the direction of universalism does not lessen but heightens the significance of this halt to stress the crucial importance of Christian proclamation. The stop is arresting not only as marking a frontier for human Christian thinking or as reminding us of the place of the Church in God's purpose, but as showing that a theology verging upon universalism can recognize as well as a theology of a different kind how urgent the task of preaching the Gospel must be.

We have now considered, very baldly it must be confessed, two contrasting types of theology, each of which is drawn towards the idea of a universal salvation. In the former human freedom is a prerequisite for real personal relationship with God, the basis of that co-operation with God or resistance to him which mark man off as a distinctive being, and, if resistance be persisted in, the reality which God must both respect and overcome in the fulfilment of his purpose to gather all men to himself in Christ. In the latter, the accent falls on a divine decision in election which indeed acknowledges man (this is more and more true of Barth's theology) but does not give a comparable status to his freedom. Despite their differences, these two theologies have one massive emphasis in common. *It is the stress upon the outgoing, world-embracing, utterly faithful, endlessly self-spending grace of God towards mankind.* This shared insight is surely derived from a prolonged look at and reflection upon the heart of the biblical message. Both are urged towards the same goal by their understanding of God.

Are we to conclude, then, that a movement towards the idea of a universal salvation is inescapable for any serious grappling with the issue of man's final destiny in the light of the revealed character of God? I believe we must. The process at work in the minds of men like Barth and Farmer is a process which we can see at work in our own minds, in so far as we are Christian. It is a process which, starting from the sovereign and universal love of God, finds it impossible

206

to come to rest save at the point where that love has won
its final triumph by gathering all to the heart of God. The
argument is built not upon the foundation of a carefully constructed catena of biblical texts but upon the view of God
which is uncovered to us by the biblical revelation. The God
who in Jesus Christ has shown himself bound to man by his
own loving will cannot allow man's sin to thwart his purpose
for ever. That is where we begin. And from this we go on
to say that because we ourselves have been and still are the
objects of God's grace and concern which he directs towards
all, we do not desire, in the end, a salvation for ourselves
in which the whole world of men does not share. We hesitate
to take Paul's words upon our lips but we understand what
was in his heart when he cried, 'I could wish that myself were
accursed from Christ for my brethren' (Rom. 9.3). In so far
as we even aspire to utter such a thought, we are aware that
in its self-sacrificing and other-centred outreach it could only
proceed from beyond our narrow selves, from God, from the
Spirit of Christ. In the third place, the movement of the
Christian mind towards the possibility of a salvation without
limit is a movement away from everlasting hell. If I may
quote Ferré again: 'Heaven to those who truly love all, can
be Heaven only when it has emptied Hell.'[13] Which of us
finds it possible to be at ease with a God who creates human
beings in such a manner that the abuse of their freedom, however terrible, is visited with unending penalty? Many
Christians, I suspect, settle the issue at the back of the mind
by accepting the idea of abiding consequences and then
limiting the duration of these consequences in the after-life.
They are, in fact, crypto-universalists. I think, for instance,
of P. T. Forsyth who, haunted as he almost was by the weight
of the holy judgement of God upon sin, could yet write during
the First World War, 'There are more conversions on the
other side than on this.'

I have spoken throughout this lecture of *a movement in
Christian thought towards universal salvation*. My own conviction

is that this movement is an echo, a reflection, a derivative of the outgoing movement of God's love. Our thought cannot help travelling in the direction in which God is going. Two things, however, must be added, each of them a reminder that as Christians we dare not look at these matters as spectators from some lofty eminence but are personally and costingly involved with our whole existence. The first is that we have no right at all to envisage or speak of a world redemption unless we ourselves are working for it with our dedicated powers. The man who talks glibly of a God who will save all without allowing himself to be caught up into the redemptive passion of God shows thereby how ill he has understood what salvation is. The second thing that must be added is that what I have called an inescapable movement within the Christian mind towards the idea of universal salvation is but a movement and is never quite out of tension with the recognition that it is a fearful thing to persist in the rejection of God. Do what we may, we cannot banish from the Christian consciousness the strong words of our Lord about fire, about darkness, about it being better for a man never to have been born. The appeal to our awful human responsibility remains. Thus the hope which Christians cannot but cherish that God in his great love will find his way ultimately to the throne of every human heart, cannot become the subject of preaching in the form of a dogma or cannot enter into preaching in a way that would diminish by one iota the answerability of the hearer as he listens to the Word of Life. But it can inform preaching as a dynamic, giving to it an insistent and urgent note of wooing that is in accord with the very spirit of the Gospel.

The tension between the Christian hope and the possibility of a continuing repudiation of God cannot be dissolved in this life. We feel that tension in ourselves and it is perhaps significant, when we reflect upon it, that when the mind dwells on the hope, it is a hope chiefly for others whereas when it dwells on the repudiation we feel we must be on our guard

lest *we* be found rejecters of God. There are two passages in
modern literature which make this point very forcibly. The
first occurs in the essay which F. D. Maurice wrote on *Eternal
Life and Eternal Death*. That essay reads now like a rather mild
protest against an easy acceptance of everlasting or as he
called it endless punishment, although it cost him his chair.

> There is one other consideration which I would impress
> very earnestly upon my brethren – especially upon the
> clergy – before I conclude. The doctrine of endless punish-
> ment is avowedly put forward as necessary for the repro-
> bates of this world, the publicans and harlots, though per-
> haps religious men might dispense with it. Now I find in
> our Lord's discourses, that when He used such words as
> these, 'Ye serpents, ye generation of vipers, how shall ye
> escape the damnation of Hell?', He was speaking to reli-
> gious men, to doctors of the Law; but that when He went
> amongst publicans and sinners, it was to preach the Gospel
> of the Kingdom of God.[14]

That is worth pondering. The other passage comes from the
chapter 'The Destiny of the Individual' in the late Dr A.
E. Taylor's first volume of Gifford Lectures, *The Faith of a
Moralist*, and has been often quoted. He concludes the discussion thus.

> A living divine was recently reported, correctly or not, to
> have declared that 'if there really are diabolical men, no
> doubt their destiny is perdition, but I should hope that
> such men are very few'. I should like myself to hope that
> there are none such, but there is just one man, of the many
> whom I have known, about whom I feel it is salutary not
> to be over-sanguine, myself.

In other words there can be no false security in the Christian
life. To take our own Christian standing and future for
granted is to take God for granted. His love is not a cushion
on which we can rest but a spur that drives us to obedient

action. Because God is a consuming fire, his love freely offered to us in Christ compels us always to give our answer in responsible freedom. That is true whether for this world or for the next, if the law of the spiritual world abides. If the Christian hope is fulfilled in God's long future it will surely be not because God has beaten down all resistance but because with the ingenuity of his tireless grace he has found a means whereby to bring about the glad and free surrender of all. Whatever new forms it may assume that means will still be what we Christians call the way of the Cross.

NOTES

1. *God and Men*, p. 144.
2. *The Christian Understanding of God*, p. 242.
3. 'What do we mean by Heaven? What do we mean by Hell?', *Essays and Addresses*, vol. I, p. 209.
4. H. H. Farmer, *God and Men*, p. 134.
5. ibid., p. 144.
6. ibid., pp. 149–50.
7. ibid., p. 150.
8. *Church Dogmatics*, IV. I, p. 113.
9. ibid., p. 103.
10. ibid., p. 100.
11. *The Triumph of Grace in the Theology of Karl Barth*, p. 295.
12. Barth, op. cit., p. 118.
13. *The Christian Understanding of God*, p. 229.
14. *Theological Essays*, p. 324.

Acknowledgements

The lectures which form the collection in this volume previously appeared in the following publications:

1. *The Idea of Immortality in Relation to Religion and Ethics* by William Temple. *Congregational Quarterly*, Vol. x, 1932, pp. 11–21.

2. *Rebirth or Immortality?* by Sydney Cave. *The Expositor*, 9th series, No. 2, Feb. 1924, pp. 103–21.

3. *The Bible and Personal Immortality* by T. W. Manson. *Congregational Quarterly*, Vol. xxxii, 1954, pp. 7–16.

4. *The Teaching of Jesus Concerning the Future Life* by H. T. Andrews. *Congregational Quarterly*, Vol. v, 1927, pp. 264–76.

5. *Immortality and Resurrection* by C. K. Barrett. *London Quarterly and Holborn Review*, April 1965, pp. 91–102.

6. *Just Men Made Perfect* by George B. Caird. *London Quarterly and Holborn Review*, April 1966, pp. 89–98.

7. *The Contribution of the Book of Revelation to the Christian Belief in Immortality* by G. R. Beasley-Murray. *Scottish Journal of Theology*, Feb. 1974, Vol. 27, pp. 76–93.

8. *God's Judgement of the Individual after Death* by H. Cunliffe-Jones. *London Quarterly and Holborn Review*, April 1967, pp. 116–28.

9. *The Hope of Glory* by H. F. Lovell Cocks. *Congregational Quarterly*, Vol. xxxiv, 1956, pp. 105–18.

10. *Heaven and Hell* by A. M. Ramsey. *Canterbury Essays and Addresses*, SPCK, 1964, pp. 32–40.

11. *Immortality and Bereavement* by Peter Barraclough. Printed privately as a pamphlet, 1970.

12. *Ultimate Triumph* by Charles S. Duthie. *Scottish Journal of Theology*, June 1961, Vol. 14, pp. 156–71.